"If you're a small-business person and can only afford one self-help law book, *Small Business Legal Smarts* is the one to buy. **An invaluable reference tool for small business owners** with legal questions, Jacobs's book fills a special niche between "do-it-yourself" legal guides and just tossing your hands up and turning everything over to your lawyer. The question and answer format allows readers to quickly find the information they need to work knowledgeably with lawyers. **No small business should be without a copy.**"

> JAMES C. TURNER
> Executive Director
> HALT—An Organization of Americans for
> Legal Reform

"Very few aspects of running a business are free from concerns with the law. But not every legal question calls for an expensive lawyer. **Deborah Jacobs's *Small Business Legal Smarts* allows small business owners to tap the practical legal know-how that can save them both time and money.** Timely. Useful. Accessible."

> EDWARD A. DAUER
> Dean Emeritus and Professor of Law
> College of Law, University of Denver

"Business owners are always trying to balance the demands on their time, and quick legal advice seldom fits into their schedules—or budgets. Deborah Jacobs makes it easy for entrepreneurs to get answers to legal questions as they arise. **This book is an essential reference for every entrepreneur's desktop.**"

> ANN DUGAN
> Director, Small Business Development Center
> Katz Graduate School of Business
> University of Pittsburgh

Small
BUSINESS
Legal
Smarts

Deborah L. Jacobs

Small
BUSINESS
Legal
Smarts

BLOOMBERG PRESS
PRINCETON

Books are available for bulk purchases at special discounts. Special editions or book excerpts can also be created to specifications. For information, please write: Special Markets Department, Bloomberg Press.

This publication contains the author's opinions and is designed to provide accurate and authoritative information. It is sold with the understanding that the author, publisher, and Bloomberg L.P. are not engaged in rendering legal, accounting, investment-planning, or other professional advice. The reader should seek the services of a qualified professional for such advice; the author, publisher, and Bloomberg L.P. cannot be held responsible for any loss incurred as a result of specific investments or planning decisions made by the reader.

First edition published 1998

1 3 5 7 9 10 8 6 4 2

Jacobs, Deborah L., 1956–
    Small business legal smarts/ Deborah L. Jacobs. --1st ed.
        p.   cm.   --(Bloomberg small business)
    Includes bibliographical references and index.
    ISBN 1-57660-020-3
    1. Small business - - Law and legislation --United States--Popular
works. I. Title. II. Series.
    KF1659.Z9J33   1998
    346.73'0652--dc21   98-19024
                                                                          CIP
Permissions and credits on page 237

ACQUIRED AND EDITED BY
Steven Gittelson

BOOK DESIGN BY
Don Morris Design

To Ken
—D.L.J.

Choosing the right company structure and anticipating
legal glitches can save you money, whether you're just
starting out or preparing to expand

Business Formats

Physical Setup

Contingency Planning

HIRING AND MANAGING EMPLOYEES.........96
Employment law basics to help prevent costly legal claims

ADR Practicalities

How to stay out of trouble with the IRS and keep
more of what you earn

Write-Offs

Taxes

Records

ACKNOWLEDGMENTS

I CAN ONLY BEGIN TO THANK THE MANY PEOPLE WHO HELPED turn the idea of this book into a reality.

Among them are the legal experts I've quoted and who were so generous with their time. But I'm also indebted to scores of others who aren't named. They include the readers and business owners who have written to me over the years and talked with me about their own legal quandaries. While I was researching this book, a number of small business organizations reached out to their memberships to help identify other key questions that company owners want answered. Thanks to the American Society of Women Entrepreneurs, National Association for the Self-Employed, National Association for the Cottage Industry, National Federation of Independent Business, and President's Resource Organization. I am grateful, too, for the help of Jennifer Cowan, my former research assistant who was never more than an e-mail away.

At Bloomberg Press, I had the pleasure of working with an exceptionally energetic and conscientious team: John Crutcher, Barbara Diez, Jack Flynn, Steven Gittelson, Lisa Goetz, Melissa Hafner, Bill Inman, Sean Kelly, Jared Kieling, Don Morris, Christina Palumbo, Priscilla Treadwell, and Mindy Weinberg. Kieling, who edited the manuscript and shepherded the book through publication, offered the perfect mix of insight, wit, and wisdom.

Finally, I would like to thank my husband, Ken Stern, who supplied unflagging enthusiasm and continues to be an inspiration.

Introduction

IF YOU'RE LIKE MANY SMALL-BUSINESS OWNERS, YOU
put off calling a lawyer until you're in deep trouble.
That's not surprising, considering the hefty fees that
many attorneys charge and their tendency to talk in
legal lingo that few people can understand.

The trouble is, small-business owners can have
big legal problems. And they need lawyers now
more than ever. More business decisions have legal
ramifications. Society is more litigious. Countless
laws tell even small firms how to run their shops.
Businesses on the leading edge use the law to their
economic advantage. Companies that don't fall
behind.

Other books will tell you how to cut costs by
doing some of the legal work yourself. But
successful business owners don't have time or
inclination to be amateur lawyers. And the stakes
are just too high if they foul up.

I wrote this book to give you another alternative.

This book is designed to get you to a lawyer in time and to help you buy only the advice you really need. It provides quick answers in plain English to the questions that arise most often. Then it tells you how to keep costs down when you consult the high-priced professionals. Think of it as a business owner's guide to consuming legal services.

That kind of advice could have saved Irving Green a lot of grief. Green, an entrepreneur in Cedarhurst, New York, spent three years and hundreds of thousands of dollars developing and marketing a CD-ROM. Then he experienced every small-business owner's nightmare: a warning letter from software behemoth Microsoft. It said that Green's CD-ROM—a $99.95 compendium of 12 books about Judaism called *The First Electronic Jewish Bookshelf*—infringed Microsoft's trademark on the word *bookshelf*. Green hadn't even thought to do a trademark search before launching his product.

Six months and reams of legal documents later,

Green reached what he calls "an amicable agreement" with Microsoft. In a way, he got off easy. His lawyer took the case on contingency, so Green could pay him from the settlement proceeds instead of incurring substantial out-of-pocket costs. And without being forced to change the product name (something that would have been "painfully expensive"), Green was able to continue selling the CD-ROM until, in time, it became out of date.

But before that happened, Green had plenty of aggravation. And he learned an important lesson for the next time. "You can't operate from the hip," he says. "You have to look at a lot of angles that the little guy doesn't ordinarily look at."

I wrote this book to help you look at many of those angles.

A lawyer who made the switch to journalism more than a dozen years ago, I've run my own small business almost ever since. As a lawyer who's also been a client, I've looked at legal problems from both sides of the desk. And I understand the practical concerns behind many legal dilemmas. I've experienced them firsthand and heard about them from the many company owners I've interviewed while covering law and business.

Organized around business issues, rather than legal ones, this book is oriented toward the practical aspects of running a company. You'll find answers to 125 questions, involving such topics as choosing the right corporate structure, protecting innovations and inventions, hiring and managing employees, and marketing products and services.

You don't need to know legal jargon to benefit from this book. Just flip to the chapter that covers a particular business matter, whether it's doing your taxes, resolving disputes, or getting paid. There you'll find the answers to questions you may already have. You'll also learn how to prevent problems you didn't even anticipate.

Along with brief answers to the questions

business owners ask most often, there are cost-saving tips, notes about opportunities to seize, and red flags of trouble. With this background, you won't have to pay a lawyer to explain things from scratch. You'll know the questions to ask, where to turn for help, and how to evaluate the advice you're hearing.

Better yet, the next time you pick up the phone to call an attorney or step into a lawyer's office, you'll be a much smarter client.

DEBORAH L. JACOBS

CHAPTER 1

Planning—or Expanding— Your Setup

I N THE FLUSH OF STARTING A COMPANY OR preparing to expand, no business owner wants to ponder all the things that could go wrong. But anticipating potential glitches that could diminish your triumphs is the best way to protect what you earn. Key items that should be on your agenda are choosing a company format, setting up your physical plant, and planning for contingencies.

When deciding how to structure a business, legal liability is often the key factor. Other concerns should also weigh into the equation, though. You'll want to think about taxes, funding, and whether you eventually hope to sell the company or hand over the reins to family.

Likewise, when choosing a location for your operations, it pays to think ahead. Whether you're dealing with local zoning rules or negotiating the terms of a lease, you'll want to be sure the physical setup allows you to do everything you've planned.

Insure against the events that could tear your venture apart, but hope that all goes well. In that case, you'll have a tidy bundle to pass along to the next generation. And it's not too soon to start some estate planning so they don't wind up with a hefty tax bill from Uncle Sam.

Business Formats

IN SETTING UP A COMPANY, YOU HAVE A CHOICE among five primary ways of operating a business. The structure you choose should depend on your potential liability, tax considerations, need for financing, and plans for succession. It is possible to change the legal structure of a business during its existence.

SHOULD I INCORPORATE?

MANY BUSINESSES RAISE THIS QUESTION because they're afraid a lawsuit could wipe them out—not just professionally, but also personally. That can be a risk for both sole proprietorships and partnerships.

In a sole proprietorship, you are the business. Therefore all your personal assets are available to pay any business debts, such as taxes or legal damages from lawsuits. The business files a tax form (Internal Revenue Service Schedule C or C-EZ) reporting income or losses. These amounts then appear on your federal income tax return and are subject to regular personal income taxes.

The same principles apply in a partnership, in which two or more owners agree to share profits and losses. Income and losses "flow through" to the individual and are taxed at the individual rate. Each partner is fully responsible for all debts and liabilities of the partnership. In other words, if your partner doesn't pay the rent or contribute to the payroll, you could be stuck with it.

As with a sole proprietorship, the major disadvantage of a partnership is that it does not protect owners from liability. One exception is a limited partnership, a costly and strictly regulated option in which only the general partners, who manage the company, are completely liable for all legal obligations; "limited partners" (essentially investors who do not participate in day-to-day management) are liable only to the extent of their investments.

Since business owners do not want to risk losing everything they have, many decide to operate as a corporation, which is a legal entity separate from its owners. This usually protects owners from the liability of the corporation. If the corporation is unable to pay its bills, for example, the creditor can only recover company assets (if any)—it can't dig into your personal bank account.

Another possibility is a relatively new business structure called a "limited-liability company," or LLC. This entity, which all states and the District of Columbia now recognize, combines the advantages of a corporation and a partnership.

SMALL BUSINESS LEGAL SMARTS

PLANNING—OR EXPANDING—YOUR SETUP

Like a corporation, the LLC protects the personal assets of owners (known as members) from liabilities of the company.

For federal tax purposes, LLCs have the option of being taxed like sole proprietorships, in the case of single-member LLCs, or like partnerships, for LLCs with two or more members. Owners pay no tax at the company level but are taxed instead on business income at their respective individual rates. That way, the LLC can avoid the problem of double taxation of shareholders inherent in a corporation *(see Q2)*. Alternatively, LLCs can choose to be taxed at the lower corporate rates, which might appeal to a company that doesn't plan to distribute dividends *(see Q2)*. To do that, you must file IRS Form 8832, Entity Classification Election *(see Q5)*.

While some states follow the federal rule, others, concerned about potential lost revenues, are levying separate taxes on limited-liability companies—just as they might do with corporations. So before you rush to choose this business format, check with a lawyer or tax accountant about the potential tax implications in your state.

Which structure should you choose? If there are a lot of startup losses and you're not concerned about liability, you might choose a flow-through entity like a sole proprietorship or a partnership. Otherwise, the LLC is the preferred entity, says Samuel Starr, a tax partner with the accounting firm of Coopers & Lybrand in Washington, D.C.

But dealing with a relatively new legal entity does carry some risks. Most notably, the limits of owners' liability haven't been widely tested in the courts, so conceivably you're not as well protected as you'd be with a corporate entity. If you need to raise money, expect commercial lenders to ask for members' personal guarantees, just as they probably would with a closely held company.

I WANT TO INCORPORATE. WHAT ARE MY OPTIONS?

THE CHOICES ARE A C-CORPORATION OR AN S-corporation. Here are the key concerns:

◆ **Tax issues.** Unlike the C-corporation, an S-corporation doesn't pay corporate tax. Instead, shareholders report the company's income—and losses—directly on their individual income-tax returns and pay tax at individual rates of up to 39.6 percent.

While corporate earnings are taxed at the lower rate of 34 percent, they get taxed twice. First the company pays corporate tax. From whatever's left, the business may pay its stockholders (including you, the business owner) a dividend. You then pay personal income tax on the dividend.

To illustrate: For every $100 of taxable income, a C-corporation pays $34 in federal taxes, leaving $66 that it can distribute to shareholders as a dividend. Assuming these owner-shareholders are in the highest tax bracket, they'd pay 39.6 percent of the dividend, or roughly $26, in personal income tax. For each $100 that the company earns, the owners have paid about $60 ($34 + $26) in taxes.

Becoming an S-corporation is one way to avoid the double tax on earnings of a C-corporation.

◆ **Anticipated losses.** If you expect large losses, you might want to operate as an S-corporation. That's because, in figuring your own taxes, you may be able to subtract the company's losses from your other income (like profits from another firm). In contrast, the losses of a C-corporation stay with the company. The business can't subtract them for tax purposes until it has a profit.

Strict rules limit the ability of S-corporation shareholders to deduct losses from taxable gains. The deduction can't be more than the adjusted basis (appreciated or depreciated book value) of the individual's investment. And the IRS requires that an owner's level of activity in the business with the loss match his or her level of activity in the firm with the profits. The test is whether you, the owner, are "materially and actively" involved in both businesses. If someone puts 500 hours or more per year into the business, he or she will probably meet that standard, says Samuel Starr.

◆ **Need for financing.** If you want to get funding from outside investors and give them shares in your company, a C-corporation provides more flexibility than an S-corporation. C-corporations can have unlimited numbers of shareholders and different classes of shareholders. The shareholders may be other corporations, individuals, or foreigners. S-corporations, in contrast, may be hindered by the rule that there be only one class of stock *(see Q3)* and by limitations on the number and type of shareholders *(see Q3)*.

HOW IS A LIMITED-LIABILITY COMPANY *(see Q1)* DIFFERENT FROM AN S-CORPORATION *(see Q2)*?

Q 3 S-CORPORATIONS HAVE BENEFITS SIMILAR TO those of LLCs but carry substantial restrictions. They may have no more than 75 shareholders, for example. Shareholders must be citizens or residents of the United States and cannot be corporations or partnerships. (Starting in 1998, they're allowed to be pensions, public charities, private foundations, and employee stock ownership plans, or ESOPs.) In contrast, the LLC can have owners of any kind (individuals, estates, corporations, partnerships) in unlimited numbers. Members can be active in management (like partners) or passive (like corporate shareholders), in which case they elect managers to run the company.

Another distinction relates to the types of ownership interests that are allowed. In an LLC there can usually be any number of types of ownership interests. An S-corporation, however, can only have one class of stock, meaning that all shares must have the same rights (for example, rights to dividends and liquidation rights); the exception is voting rights, which may differ. Therefore, the LLC has an advantage over the S-corporation in attracting investors.

13

HOW DO SUCCESSION PLANS INFLUENCE THE CHOICE OF A BUSINESS STRUCTURE?

Q 4 OF THE AVAILABLE CHOICES, THE C-CORPORATION, limited-liability company, and partnership are the most enduring and the most flexible. With the latter two, most state laws provide that the business is automatically dissolved upon the death or resignation of a partner (or member), but the remaining partners (or members) can vote to continue it. With a C-corporation, there's no such formality; since it's a separate legal entity, it survives the death of a shareholder, and stock can be sold or transferred at any time without dissolving the corporation.

If it's important that your business survive your death, don't operate as a sole proprietorship. While an owner can always transfer ownership by bequeathing the business assets, the company officially dissolves upon the founder's death, with assets becoming part of his or her estate.

Likewise, if you're running a family-owned company and want to keep it that way, you should avoid doing business as an S-corporation. Various restrictions on these corporate entities *(see Q3)* make them tricky vehicles for estate planning, which is an important part of passing a company along to future generations *(see Q15)*.

WHAT IS INVOLVED IN FORMING VARIOUS BUSINESS STRUCTURES—A PARTNERSHIP, LIMITED-LIABILITY COMPANY, AND A CORPORATION?

A PARTNERSHIP IS FORMED THROUGH AN ORAL or a written agreement. The format can be enormously flexible with respect to the numbers of partners, allocations of income, and who or what can be considered partners.

To form a limited-liability company, a business files articles of organization with the state, providing basic information about the business. A separate document, known as the operating agreement, outlines the rules for managing the firm. The cost of having a lawyer do this paperwork can range from $1,500 to $5,000.

Forming a corporation involves substantial paperwork, including filing articles of incorporation and paying a state filing fee (about $100 to $150). The company also must have a board of directors to manage it and bylaws to govern its operations. Although you can do at least part of the paperwork yourself, you're likely to need a lawyer to help you get started (in some states, a lawyer is required). Such legal assistance usually costs between $500 and $2,000.

Once the corporation is formed, its owners must comply with certain formalities in day-to-day management of the company. These include maintaining separate accounts for corporate funds, carefully recording corporate transactions, and consulting members of the board of directors about important decisions.

TIP: If you formed a limited-liability company after January 1, 1997, you may have an extra piece of paperwork—IRS Form 8832, Entity Classification Election. Under the IRS "Check-the-Box" rules, if you don't file this form, the IRS will presume you should pay federal tax as a partnership (if there are two or more owners) or as a sole proprietorship (for single-owner entities). Alternatively, you can check the box indicating you want to be taxed as a corporation *(see Q1)*. Your "election" to be treated as a corporation instead is effective when you file the form, unless you specify a different date (which can't be more than 75 days before or 12 months after you file Form 8832). This form must also be attached to the company's tax return for the year it's effective or, if the business isn't required to file a return that year, to one of the owner's returns.

TIP: Forming a business entity is a big step with long-term consequences. Therefore, you shouldn't do it without professional advice *(for more about legal self-help materials, see Q40)*. The stakes are too high if you make a mistake. And chances are, your time is much better spent perfecting and marketing your product or service. But if you want to ponder the do-it-yourself option—or just read more about various entities—there are a growing number of books on the subject. Here are some that I recommend:

How to Form Your Own California Corporation; How to Form Your Own New York Corporation; and *How to Form Your Own Texas Corporation,* all written by Anthony Mancuso and published by Nolo Press ($39.95 each), explain incorporation basics. They are accompanied by software to help you form your own corporation. *How to Form Your Own California Corporation* is also available without software ($29.95).

The Partnership Book, by Denis Clifford and Ralph Warner, includes forms and a disk that you can use to do some of the legal work yourself (Nolo Press, $34.95).

How to Form Your Own Limited Liability Company, by

Anthony Mancuso, is a guide to getting started with this relatively new legal entity (Nolo Press, $24.95).

WHY MIGHT I WANT TO SWITCH THE FORMAT OF MY COMPANY?

BUSINESSES GO THROUGH PHASES, AND different formats may be appropriate for various stages in a company's life cycle. During a growth stage, perhaps you'd prefer to be a C-corporation, making it easier to get outside financing. Once your business is generating a lot of income, you may want to return to the S-corporation format so you don't wind up paying double tax *(see Q2)*.

Converting from a partnership to a C-corporation or limited-liability company poses few problems, as does switching from a sole proprietorship or partnership to a LLC. Converting from a C-corporation to a partnership, sole proprietorship, or LLC, however, involves liquidating the C-corporation. Owners (shareholders) are then taxed on the gain of any appreciated asset of the corporation.

Getting in and out of an S-corporation is even more difficult. Firms that elect S status may, under certain circumstances, be taxed on gains in the value of assets that were owned before the S election. If they revoke their S status to become a C-corporation or some other business format, they cannot reelect S status for five years.

Because of the tax pitfalls and restrictions involved, business owners should seek professional advice when considering any change in business structure. Here are the key issues you'll want to discuss:

◆ Taxes
◆ Financing
◆ Administrative expense and hassle
◆ Succession
◆ Ease of converting to another entity.

(See "Business Formats at a Glance" on pages 18–19.)

HOW DO I CHANGE MY COMPANY NAME?

 MANY STATES REQUIRE THAT A CORPORATE NAME be registered so that regulators can be sure there aren't several businesses operating with the same name. To change the corporate name, then, you usually fill out a simple change of name form, something that you can do without the help of an attorney.

Separate from this state law issue is the question of whether your name has any trademark value because it distinguishes your goods or services from other companies' *(see introductions to Chapter 2 and to Q27)*. If so, you can register the name for federal trademark protection, which entitles you to stop others from adopting or using it *(see Q27)*. Registering a trademark requires a search to see whether another business is already using the name *(see Q27)*. You must also complete the registration form required by the U.S. Patent and Trademark Office *(see Q27)*.

I'VE CHOSEN A BUSINESS FORMAT. NOW I'M THINKING ABOUT BUYING A FRANCHISE. HOW DO I AVOID GETTING BURNED?

 WHAT YOU GET WITH A FRANCHISE IS AN INSTANT business with name recognition that could attract customers. What you don't get is any guarantee of ever seeing a profit.

Unfortunately, federal and state rules don't prevent many widespread practices that, in effect, keep franchisees from operating in the black: opening a competing unit nearby, imposing onerous terms when the contract's up for renewal, and forcing franchisees to buy supplies at greatly inflated prices. Here are some ways to avoid getting burned:

◆ **Take a hard look at the industry, the community, and the company.** Before starting any business, you need to think about whether there's a lasting market for the product or service. All the more so with franchises, where the typical contract can run from 10 to 20 years.

Then scout for a company that's profitable and was in business at least 5 to 10 years before it started selling franchises, says Susan Kezios, president of the consumer-oriented

Business Formats at a Glance

KEY FEATURES OF THE PRIMARY BUSINESS ENTITIES

BUSINESS STRUCTURE	SOLE PROPRIETORSHIP	PARTNERSHIP
Number of owners	1 person.	2 or more people; flexible about who or what they may be.
Method of formation	No special steps are required.	Verbal contract is sufficient, but a written agreement is advisable.
Legal liability	Owner has unlimited liability.	General partners have unlimited liability. Limited partners are liable to the extent of their investments.
Tax liability	Owner is liable.	Partners are liable, whether or not profits are distributed.
Tax rate	Owner is taxed at individual rate of up to 39.6 percent.	Partners are taxed at individual rate of up to 39.6 percent.
Transfer of part ownership	Fully transferable through sale or transfer of company assets.	May require consent of all partners.
Deciding factors	Not concerned about liability and eager to keep setup costs down.	Two or more owners not concerned about liability.

C-CORPORATION	S-CORPORATION	LIMITED-LIABILITY COMPANY
Any number; flexible about who or what they may be.	Maximum of 75, with restrictions on who or what they may be.	Any number; flexible about who or what they may be.
Requirements set by state law.	Requirements set by state and federal law.	Requirements set by state law.
Shareholders are protected from personal liability.	Shareholders are protected from personal liability.	Members (owners) are protected from personal liability.
Corporation is liable.	Shareholders are liable, whether or not profits are distributed.	Members (owners) are liable, whether or not profits are distributed.
Corporation is taxed at corporate rate of up to 34 percent.	Shareholders are taxed at individual rate of up to 39.6 percent.	Members (owners) are taxed at individual rate of up to 39.6 percent.
Shares are freely transferable.	Transfer of shares may affect S-status.	Generally requires consent of all members (owners).
Ease of attracting investors.	Want traditional route of limiting liability while avoiding double tax.	Willing to use a relatively new entity that combines the best features of a corporation and a partnership.

American Franchisee Association, in Chicago. Choose one that's been franchising for several years.

◆ **Read the franchisor's disclosure papers.** Federal Trade Commission rules require franchisors to supply you with specific information about what you're getting into. You'll find it in a hefty document called the "Franchise Offering Circular." Among other things, it has to include a financial statement, tell you about charges to start and continue the franchise, and give you names of current franchisees. Most companies make no claims on paper about earnings you can expect (they're worried about lawsuits by franchisees who fall short).

◆ **Tally up the expenses.** Your costs begin with the one-time up-front fee that you pay to the franchisor (from $5,000 for a home-based franchise to $150,000 for a fast-food joint in a shopping center), says Ann Dugan, a former franchisee, who is now director of the Small Business Development Center at the University of Pittsburgh. Add to that equipment purchases; renting, buying, or building a storefront; and cash for everyday expenses like inventory, supplies, and utility bills. Whether or not you're making a profit, you'll have to pay the franchisor's yearly royalty fee (typically between 5 and 15 percent) plus advertising charges (3 to 8 percent), both based on gross (not net) revenues.

◆ **Talk to other franchisees.** Some questions to ask each of them: How have your earnings compared with what you expected? Did the contract and disclosure documents accurately describe your relationship with the franchisor? How effective has the franchisor's advertising been in bringing you business? Have you had occasion to renew the franchise agreement (if so, were there any problems)?

◆ **Consult the pros.** Before you sign on the dotted line, you'll want a good accountant to examine the offering circular and a lawyer to scrutinize the circular and contract. Franchise agreements tend to be "take it or leave it" propositions; your lawyer isn't going to have much luck customizing its provisions for you, so don't expect to pay for a lot of detailed negotiations. Which is not to say you shouldn't buy a franchise—just go into it with your eyes open. Chances are you're not buying a cash cow. More likely, you're buying yourself a job. And it can be a very low-paying one at that.

TIP: To review the franchise agreement, choose an attorney who chiefly represents franchisees. The American Franchisee Association (312-431-0545) can provide referrals.

Physical Setup

BEFORE MAKING COSTLY COMMITMENTS ABOUT WHERE YOU operate your business, check the local zoning rules and the fine print on any lease you're thinking of signing. No matter how inflexible a situation seems, many terms are negotiable.

HOW CAN I DEAL WITH POTENTIAL ZONING RESTRICTIONS?

IT'S BEST TO CHECK LOCAL ORDINANCES BEFORE starting or expanding your operation. They're usually available free (or for a nominal charge) at the town hall or through any other local entity in charge of zoning (it might be called the department of planning, buildings, or zoning).

Specific restrictions vary from place to place, and there are endless variations on the theme, says Jim Schwab, editor of *Zoning News*, the monthly newsletter of the Chicago-based American Planning Association. Assuming your home is in a residential district (as opposed to one zoned for homes and businesses), you should focus on rules about residential uses.

The first thing to look for is anything that specifically permits or prohibits your type of business. Many controls stem from concerns about traffic and parking, Schwab says. Rules about noise and odors are also very common.

While some ordinances include laundry lists of what you can and can't do, others are far broader. Vague definitions of "home occupation" or "professional uses" may leave you wondering how to characterize your interior decorating or advertising business. Potentially more troublesome are rules about how much of the house your business can occupy, the number of nonfamily members you can employ there, and the quantities of inventory you're allowed to store.

Sometimes the code permits you to run a business only if you meet specific conditions. These might include requirements to provide off-street parking or landscape your yard to screen neighbors from clients' comings and goings. With such so-called "conditional uses," the code says what you must do to make your business legal.

In contrast are cases where the law requires a special-use permit. Here local officials interpret the zoning code to decide what conditions you must meet. If you get the go-ahead, they'll be spelled out in a permit. You don't necessarily need a lawyer for this process.

When should you hire a lawyer? You need one if the code is unclear and you're asking for a ruling about what you can and can't do. You'll also want a pro to help with the even touchier subject of variances—exemptions from the zoning rules.

To get a variance, you generally have to show that without one the property has "unique physical conditions that prevent you from getting a reasonable return on your investment," says Elise Wagner, a lawyer with Battle Fowler in New York City. But you can't get a variance for what's known as a "self-imposed hardship." For instance, an argument that you bought the house expecting to use it as a home office (but without checking the zoning) wouldn't wash, Wagner says.

Considering how vulnerable you are when the law isn't clearly on your side, you might be tempted to just keep the operation under wraps. Yet running a business illegally can raise other problems. Let's say the law requires that you add a separate entrance or install sprinklers before operating a home day care center. If you haven't complied and your house is damaged by fire, your insurer might not cover the loss, Wagner says.

Nor do neighbors like surprises at zoning board hearings. If you've kept your business a secret until then, they may "have all sorts of wild ideas about what you're doing" and imagine that it's much worse than it really is, Jim Schwab says. For that reason, he suggests you tell neighbors about the variance you want and get community members on your side before any hearings. Neighborly gestures, like running an open house or holding a block club meeting, can go a long way toward mollifying objections.

Finally, if you're operating that business out of a rental property, or the co-op or condo that you own, you'll also want to check the house rules. Even if the zoning ordinance permits your business, rules of the roost may pose another hurdle. So it's best to get the go-ahead from your landlord, co-op, or condo.

WHAT ARE THE KEY TERMS IN AN OFFICE LEASE?

FIRST DECIDE WHAT KIND OF SPACE YOU WANT and how long you need it for. Then prepare to negotiate the following key points, says Mitchell Gilbert, a lawyer with Windels, Marx, Davies & Ives in New York City.

1 **Rent.** You need to consider not just the base rent (usually calculated by square foot) but also periodic increases in the landlord's costs that you may have to share. These "escalation charges" typically include increases in (or percentages of) real estate taxes and operating expenses (such as payroll, insurance, fuel, and legal fees).

TIP: The landlord may calculate your share of operating expense escalations or use a "porter's wage formula"—tying the rent hike to the rise in union wages. You can negotiate both the charges and when they kick in.

2 **Measurement.** Have your own space planner or architect measure the area you're renting, rather than relying on the landlord's calculations. Your goal is to figure out how much usable ("carpetable") space there is. Chances are the landlord's numbers include a "loss factor": common areas (like hallways, bathrooms, electrical closets, and elevator shafts) that you can't use as office space but which are included in your square footage.

Knowing the loss factor will help you compare different alternatives and shop for the best deal: in one building it might be 20 percent, while it's 30 percent in another. In effect, space priced at $25 a square foot winds up costing more like $30 or $33.

TIP: There's some loss factor in every rental, and it's perfectly appropriate to share it with the landlord. If you don't know what it is, though, you may wind up with less floor space than you really need.

3 **Occupancy date.** Unless you're taking the premises "as is," some landlords are reluctant to name a move-in date. The less flexibility you have about when you can or must move, the more important it is that you pin them down. If the landlord can't deliver within a certain period (say, three or six months), you should have the right to terminate the lease and find other space.

4 **Renovations.** Many landlords will either contribute to the cost of your renovations or do the improvements themselves (depending on your negotiating power). A local lawyer specializing in commercial leases can tell you what landlords in your area customarily pay for.

5 **Utilities.** From your perspective, the best way to buy gas and electricity is to have them directly metered by the utility, but this may be tough for a small business to negotiate. More likely, utilities will be included in the rent or submetered by the landlord. In either case, the landlord will probably buy these services at a discount and charge a markup. That's okay, as long as what you wind up paying isn't more than you'd spend buying utilities directly. If your landlord submeters utilities, your lease should give you the right to audit claims about how much you're using.

6 **Services.** You'll want to make clear what the landlord is going to provide and what will cost extra. Topics to cover include: hot and cold water; heating, ventilation, and air-conditioning (including evenings and weekends, if you need it); cleaning; a downstairs reception desk, if any; passenger and freight elevators; and security.

7 **Repairs and maintenance.** Depending on the building, either you or the landlord may be best suited to make routine

repairs in mechanical systems, electrical systems, and plumbing. But how about building-wide improvements? For instance, during your lease, government regulations may require some drastic changes or your landlord may decide to make capital improvements. To avoid surprise charges, clearly define each party's obligations before you sign on the dotted line.

8 **Liability.** This includes possible limits on your personal liability and who should be responsible if the premises are destroyed by fire or casualty.

9 **Nondisturbance agreement.** This is a promise that your landlord gets from the bank holding the building mortgage. It prevents the lender from automatically kicking you out if the landlord defaults. A nondisturbance agreement gives you the right to remain as long as you continue to pay rent and otherwise honor the lease.

10 **Assignment and subletting.** Let's say you need to move out before the lease is up—either because your business isn't going well or because it's booming and there's no room to expand your present setup. You can cover these contingencies by reserving the right to *assign* the lease or *sublet* the premises. With an assignment, you generally turn all responsibilities over to another tenant (in some states you might remain liable yourself, though). In a sublet, you remain liable under the lease but find a tenant of your own to occupy the space and pay you rent. Without these rights, you might (again, depending on the state) get stuck paying all the rent until the lease is up.

11 **Renewal or termination.** Assuming all goes well, you may want an option to renew the lease or expand your space when the term is up. Sometimes the landlord reserves the right to end it before then. Given the toll termination could take on your business, you ought to negotiate various safeguards. Examples: how much notice the landlord must provide; reimbursement for your moving costs; and compensation for disrupting your business.

WHAT ARE THE KEY TERMS OF A RETAIL STORE OR SHOPPING CENTER LEASE?

Q 11 MANY OF THE SAME PRINCIPLES RELEVANT TO negotiating office space *(see Q10)* also apply here. One of the major differences is that retail premises are usually rented on what's called a "net lease" basis, meaning that the tenant arranges for most of its services *(see Q10)*. Unless your premises are tied to the building's mechanical systems (in which case the landlord may provide heating or air-conditioning), most such services are your responsibility.

Another important point to negotiate is what you're allowed to use the space for, says Ellen Sinreich, a New York City real estate lawyer. The broader the definition, the better, she says: if you've leased the space to sell vintage clothing, for instance, and business lags, you'll have the option of opening an ice cream parlor instead. The breadth of your use clause will also affect your ability to assign your lease or sublet the premises *(see Q10)*.

In addition, it's a good idea to get what's called a restrictive covenant, prohibiting the landlord from leasing space in the same building or nearby to a business that competes with you. How far this provision should extend will depend on where you operate. In a suburban area, it might be a mile or two; in the city, it might just cover a few blocks.

With shopping center leases, you may face additional charges for maintenance of common areas and your landlord's marketing efforts. Also consider who are the "anchor" tenants—large enterprises like K-Mart and Home Depot that generate the most traffic. You'll want to think about how viable these businesses are and how vulnerable you'll be if one or more of them leaves.

TIP: Whether you're operating in a shopping center or in some other retail space, Sinreich recommends you cover the subject of signs early on. Premature as it may sound, it's best to get the landlord's approval of the color, size, and content of your signs before you enter into the lease. Without proper signs, you may have no visibility and no customers.

DO I NEED A LAWYER FOR LEASE NEGOTIATIONS?

 UNTIL YOU AND THE LANDLORD HAVE AGREED on basic economic terms, there's not much for a lawyer to do. Before launching your search for space, though, you might want to get an initial one- or two-hour legal consultation to discuss specific issues that could apply to your situation.

Once you've chosen one or two spaces, it's time to negotiate. You can cover many of the important issues yourself, including assignment and subletting *(see Q10)*, occupancy date *(see Q10)*, and which renovations the landlord will do or pay for *(see Q10)*. When you've reached an agreement, or are very close to one, get the lawyer involved again to help put all the terms in writing.

Contingency Planning

SO MUCH TIME, ENERGY, AND MONEY GOES INTO STARTING and running a business. Yet at times it all seems very fragile. Begin planning now for ordinary human events that could have extraordinary consequences for the company you've built.

HOW CAN MY FAMILY BUSINESS AVOID HOSTILE BREAKUPS?

 THERE ARE SOME PREVENTIVE MEASURES TO consider—either when setting up the business or once trouble arises.

◆ **Create a corporate democracy.** The more family members you involve in major decisions, the greater your chances of keeping the peace, says Harold M. Hoffman, a lawyer with Kronish, Lieb, Weiner & Hellman in New York City, who helps families prevent and resolve conflicts. Instead of governing by a straight majority, Hoffman suggests you aim for at least a two-thirds vote (known as a "supermajority") or even unanimous consent for important actions. You can also use a hybrid approach, where a majority of the board of directors oversees day-to-day operations, but more significant decisions (like approving a sale or a merger or increasing the number of authorized shares) require a supermajority or unanimous vote.

◆ **Issue different classes of stock.** One common source of friction is when family members who don't work for the company have a say over how other family members run it. You can avoid such problems by creating different classes of stock, so that the people with the voting power are those who actually do the work. For instance, you might give voting stock to family members employed by the corporation, but nonvoting stock to nonemployee shareholders.

FYI: *Staying Wealthy: Strategies for Protecting Your Assets,* by Brian H. Breuel (Bloomberg Press) includes an extensive discussion of succession in a family business. *(See Problems 18–25, and Problem 46.)*

◆ **Use a buy-sell agreement.** Ordinary human events (like death, disability, retirement, or divorce) can force one family member out of the business and leave others unwilling associates. Rather than waiting for these occasions, it's best to cover all contingencies in a buy-sell agreement. Here business owners decide, when everybody is coolheaded, what happens to the shares when life interferes with business. Owners can agree to buy out each other (a "cross-purchase agreement") or to have their shares sold back to the corporation (a "redemption agreement").

Other restrictions on stock transfers can prevent majority shareholders from selling out to newcomers, Hoffman says. With a "take along" provision, for example, majority shareholders agree not to sell unless they also offer their stock to minority shareholders on the same terms. The reverse is called a "come along": you provide that, if the majority have found a buyer, the minority must sell—again on the same terms. Essentially, then, you prevent the minority from blocking a sale.

Funding methods include a payback over time so, for instance, the surviving business owner can use profits to pay off the obligation. Life insurance is another popular option, although it only helps with transfers that occur when someone dies.

Two caveats if you go this last route, advises Jonathan Blattmachr, a lawyer with Milbank, Tweed, Hadley & McCloy in New York City and a specialist in family businesses. When the company buys the policy (as it would for a redemption agreement), the proceeds may be subject to creditors' claims and to the corporate alternative minimum tax. When shareholders buy the policy on each others' lives (as they might for a cross-purchase agreement), they'll want to cover themselves in case the business falls apart before the policy comes due.

For example, let's say you work for the family enterprise and a cousin plans to buy out your shares if you die. What if the business goes bust or your relative leaves first? Be sure you've provided that you or your family will get back the insurance policy on your life, Blattmachr says.

These and other potential complications make it wise not to go it alone when drafting a buy-sell agreement. It's better to enlist a few hours of help from an experienced small-business accountant or lawyer.

TIP: The buy-sell agreement should also include a method for valuing shares. You can specify the value in advance and agree to reset it each year. Other options: use book value (net worth); a combination of book value and historic earnings; or agree to have an independent appraisal in the future.

◆ **Form a board of advisers.** This relatively new device is quickly catching on with family-owned businesses. Unlike the board of directors, a board of advisers doesn't make decisions on behalf of the company. Instead, members act as expert neutrals who can help the family get along. The board of advisers might include lawyers, bankers, accountants, and even psychologists. When push comes to shove, they can cushion the blows.

WHEN DO I NEED TO EXECUTE A POWER OF ATTORNEY?

Q 14 IF YOU ANTICIPATE NOT BEING ABLE TO RUN your business because of illness or an extended absence, you should authorize someone to handle affairs in your place. This can be done by signing a legal document known as a power of attorney. It names the person you choose as your agent (that is, your "attorney in fact") with legal authority to act on your behalf. Your agent may be a lawyer, but doesn't have to be. You can name anyone you trust and even split the power of attorney between two people (for example, your spouse and a business associate). If you name two people, you might want to require that they agree on any course of action taken in your absence.

The authority you grant may be limited to, say, handling a particular business deal while you're out of touch, or it may be broad enough to cover any matter relating to your business.

HOW DO I MINIMIZE ESTATE TAXES IN MY FAMILY-OWNED BUSINESS?

Q 15 AS WITH ALL ESTATE PLANNING, THE GOAL IS TO reduce the government's share of what you leave behind. Much depends on when and how you give assets away. The longer you wait, the more options you may foreclose.

You'll need the pros to help you decide what's best, and each lawyer or financial consultant seems to have his or her pet techniques. Choose an adviser who specializes in estate planning for small businesses. You can cut down on how long this professional must spend (and the bill you pay for counseling time) by sorting out your priorities in advance: whether you want to sell the business, for instance; which family members will run the enterprise; and who will retain an ownership interest but without any day-to-day control.

Here are some popular estate planning devices:

◆ **Create a trust when you start the business.** Before you make the first nickel, put company stock in trust for the benefit of family members, Blattmachr advises. You retain day-to-day control of the operation but have given away non-voting shares, which can appreciate. By the time you die, your family may have valuable property, which isn't considered part of your estate.

◆ **Give away money each year.** If your business is well underway but you're just starting to think about estate tax issues, a great (and easy) way to begin is by giving away, to as many heirs or other beneficiaries as you can afford, $10,000 per person (adjusted for inflation) every year. These yearly "gifts" are completely tax free, and you and your spouse are each allowed to make them to as many people as you want. In addition, each of you can currently transfer a total of $625,000 during your life and at death free of federal estate and gift tax. Under the 1997 Taxpayer Relief Act, this "unified credit" gradually increases to $1 million in the year 2006:

YEAR	CREDIT
1999	$650,000
2000 and 2001	675,000
2002 and 2003	700,000
2004	850,000
2005	950,000
2006 and later	1,000,000

Some company owners qualify for an additional exclusion, enabling them to give away up to $1.3 million worth of business interests tax free. This "family-owned business exclusion" equals the difference between the unified credit and $1.3 million, so as the unified credit goes up, the family-owned business exclusion in effect diminishes. In 1999, for instance, when the unified credit is $650,000, the family-owned business exclusion enables you to pass another $650,000 tax-free ($1.3 million minus $650,000). By 2006, the family-owned business exclusion is worth $300,000 ($1.3 million minus $1 million).

Still, a number of restrictions apply before the family-owned business exclusion kicks in:

1 The business must constitute more than half your estate.

2 Your family must own at least 30 percent of the business (50 percent in some cases).

3 You or your family must operate the business for at least five of the eight years before you die. What's more, your heirs must continue to hold and operate the company for ten years after you die; if they don't, they could lose the exclusion and have to pay estate tax on the business interests you transferred.

◆ **Form a grantor-retained annuity trust (or GRAT).** Basically, this is a technique for retaining part of the value of a business, converting it into a cash flow stream, and shifting future appreciation to the kids at a reduced cost.

Here's how it works. You put assets (such as stock or real estate) into a trust and retain the right to receive income from the trust (say a certain percentage of what the business earns) for a set period (like five or ten years). After that, the children (or whoever you name as beneficiaries) get the assets. Most important, you've taken the property out of your estate and "frozen" its value, for gift tax purposes, at a greatly discounted rate. The discount reflects the fact that the beneficiaries don't get the property right away.

Figuring the discount involves a complex actuarial calculation based on monthly interest rates that the IRS provides (the "assumed discount rate"). The higher the interest rate, the bigger the discount, and the more you stand to gain from a GRAT.

GRATs work best when there's going to be a lot of appreciation in the value of a company, says Evelyn Capassakis, director of estate planning at Coopers & Lybrand in New York City. Plus, two other factors need to work in your favor. You must outlive the term of the trust. And actual income and appreciation of the assets should be more than the assumed discount rate. If you can beat the market rate of return, you can transfer property with little or no gift tax.

◆ **Put assets in a charitable remainder trust.** This method works well for owners who anticipate selling the company and want to avoid paying capital gains tax, says Capassakis. In anticipation of the sale you create a trust, into which you then put the proceeds of the sale. During your life or the lives of certain family members, the trust pays either a fixed dollar amount from these proceeds or a portion of the company's sale price. When you or the family members die, what's left goes to charity. Even if the charity's interest isn't worth much, the trust is a tax-exempt entity, so there's no capital gains tax on the proceeds of the sale.

◆ **Form a family limited partnership.** This is an ordinary partnership, where you put some portion of your property into the partnership and transfer a limited-partnership interest to your children or others. Since you retain control of the business, the limited-partnership interests are discounted for gift tax purposes, says Capassakis. Therefore, family members wind up paying less tax than if you gave them active control over the business during your lifetime or waited until you died to transfer an interest in the business.

This estate planning technique would be appropriate for a business owner who wants to continue to control the company for awhile but at the same time give away some equity to his or her family, Capassakis says. Because it creates different classes of stock, it's not an option for S-corporations, however *(see Q3)*.

WHAT KIND OF INSURANCE DO I NEED?

Q 16 SOMETIMES THERE'S NO CHOICE BECAUSE THE law or a third party says you must carry a certain kind of insurance. For instance, most states require you to carry workers' compensation insurance to protect people injured on the job. Take a mortgage on the building where your company is located, and the bank will demand that you get property insurance.

In choosing other coverage, business owners must weigh the cost of insurance against the likely risks. Just what those risks are will depend on the type of business you're running, where you operate (juries in some states, such as Texas and California, are more "pro-plaintiff" than in others), the possibility that one disaster or lawsuit will wipe you out, and how well you can address the risks without insurance.

Here are some of the most common types of coverage businesses ought to consider:

◆ **Property.** This applies to your work space and what's in it, including furniture, inventory, equipment, and routine documents. At a minimum, the policy should protect against basic losses, like those from fire or lightning. Insuring against other kinds of losses or "perils" (such as damage from leaks, vandalism, and smoke) may require a special endorsement (or rider) at extra cost. You'll need separate policies for flood insurance (available from the federal government's National Flood Insurance Program) or earthquakes, if you face those risks.

◆ **Crime.** These may be crimes committed by your staff or others, including burglary, theft, robbery, and forgery. Depending on the risks, your options include buying bonds for your own employees or what's called a "3D" policy (for dishonesty, disappearance, and destruction), covering insiders and outsiders.

◆ **Boiler and machinery.** Though the name is a bit of a misnomer, these policies (sometimes called "equipment breakdown" or "mechanical breakdown" coverage) pay to fix machines and electrical equipment after sudden or accidental breakdowns. The policy may also cover property loss, business interruption, and the expense of expediting repairs.

◆ **Business interruption.** Consider this coverage if you're vulnerable to risks that could substantially diminish your production or temporarily put you out of business. As a rule, the interruption must stem from some kind of property damage (like a fire on your premises that requires you to shut down the store or blocks your access to business equipment)—as opposed to your own disability. Until you're up and running again, this policy will reimburse you for fixed costs, such as payroll, rent, and profit loss.

◆ **Liability.** When something you do (or don't do) in the course of your work causes injury to other people or damage to their property, you may be legally liable. And even if you win such a lawsuit, it could be expensive to defend. Liability insurance covers you for these costs and the risk of a verdict against you.

This insurance can take the form of a comprehensive or commercial general liability policy or be included as part of a business-owner's policy *(see Q17)*. But here, as with all policies, you'll want to pay attention to what's covered and what's not. If you advertise your product or service, be sure the policy covers what's called "advertising injury." This includes copyright claims based on your labels, packaging, and catalogues. Workers' compensation, claims from pollution, and damage done by a business vehicle are typically excluded.

Professionals, such as doctors, lawyers, and accountants, need professional liability (or malpractice) insurance covering mistakes for which they would be legally liable. Errors and omissions policies, appropriate for insurance agents and travel agents, cover similar types of risks.

◆ **Key employee life insurance.** This is coverage to consider if one or more employees are so essential to your business that their death would hurt your bottom line. The policy provides for a payout to the company if any of these people die.

◆ **Disability.** Designed to help you meet your expenses if you can't work because of accident or illness, disability insurance coverage depends on what you earn. The goal is not to replace your entire income but to sustain you while you're out of work. Most policies permit you to get a benefit of only 50 to 70 percent of your monthly earnings.

TIP: Don't skimp on disability insurance. If you're between 35 and 65 years old, your chances of being disabled are greater than your chances of dying, according to The National Association of Life Underwriters, a trade group. For many small-business owners, the financial implications could be devastating.

FYI: *Insuring Your Business,* by Sean Mooney (Insurance Information Institute Press, $22.50), is a comprehensive guide to insurance for the small-business owner.

ARE THERE SPECIAL INSURANCE POLICIES FOR SMALL BUSINESSES?

YES, SAYS SEAN MOONEY, A SENIOR VICE president and economist with the Insurance Information Institute in New York City. The business-owner's policy (or BOP) is the industry's attempt to cover

Insurance Shopping Tips

YOU'RE IN THE BEST POSITION to know the ins and outs of your business. So before meeting with a consultant, lawyer, or insurance agent, it pays to do some homework. Make a list of the property you might want to insure, including the estimated replacement cost (*see Q18*) of each item. Then prepare a brief description of your daily business activities and the risks you face. George A. Vaka, a lawyer with Fowler, White, Gillen, Boggs, Villareal and Banker in Tampa, Florida, offers the following additional advice to small companies shopping for insurance:

◆ Look for an agent or broker with the designation "CPCU" (Chartered Property and Casualty Underwriter), granted by the American Institute of Property and Liability Underwriters. It means that the individuals have passed a series of exams and have a good idea of the types of policies and the risks they cover.

◆ Inquire whether the agent you're working with is "captive," meaning that he or she only sells insurance for one company. You may get a better deal from an "independent"—someone who sells for a number of different carriers. To find one near you, contact the Independent Insurance Agents of America at 800-221-7917.

◆ If agents or brokers use the term "full coverage," ask them to explain what they mean. All policies have some exclusions—situations, conditions, or circumstances that aren't covered.

◆ Read the policy to see what it covers or excludes. Policies that use the term "all risks" can be confusing: typically they cover everything except what's specifically excluded. The alternative is a "named perils" policy, which covers the risks listed on the policy but no others. When in doubt, ask the agent or consultant you're working with to confirm in writing that the policy (including any special endorsements) covers the risks you're concerned about.

many of the predictable risks that a small-business owner might face. These policies combine several kinds of coverage in one package and generally cost less than each type of coverage purchased separately. They typically include theft (though not by employees), liability, property loss *(see Q16)*, and business interruption *(see Q16)*.

The cost of the policy, which usually runs between $1,000 and $3,000 a year, depends on your revenues, where your business is located, and sometimes the number of square feet that you occupy, Mooney says. As with other policies, these have exclusions, such as employment-related practices (for instance, sex, race, or age discrimination) and pollution lawsuits. You'll pay extra for special options, like covering employee theft and costly boiler breakdowns. Business-owner's policies typically don't cover consultants but are well suited to retail stores, small manufacturers, and even fast-food restaurants whose exposure fits within the policy's coverage limits, Mooney says.

For businesses not covered by the BOP, inquire through trade associations whether an insurance company or broker has put together a deal with your particular kind of business in mind. So-called "risk retention groups," which you can find the same way, may be another option. These are small businesses with similar potential liability (say a group of doctors or pest controllers) that form their own trust to distribute the risk among their members. This kind of coverage generally costs less than policies bought through a large insurer, though they may not offer as much protection.

Home-based businesses should ask about adding endorsements to the basic homeowners policy. It may be possible to cover business equipment (like computers and fax machines) and liability for injuries to clients who meet with you at home, Mooney says.

WHAT'S THE DIFFERENCE BETWEEN "REPLACEMENT COST" AND "ACTUAL CASH VALUE"?

A POLICY THAT COVERS REPLACEMENT COST WILL pay to replace something (say a building, inventory, or equipment) at today's prices. Actual cash value

gives you the value of what you've lost minus depreciation.
Let's say your fax machine, purchased two years ago for
$1,000, is destroyed by fire. A policy based on replacement
cost will give you what you'd pay to buy the same (or equivalent) machine today. If your policy paid actual cash value,
you'd get the depreciated value of the machine, which might
be just $500.

For property that becomes obsolete, like computers, fax
machines, and other electronic equipment, it generally
makes sense to cover replacement cost, Mooney says. One
exception: if you might eventually hire an outside firm to
perform services you used the equipment to perform in-
house; in that case, you'd want a lower-priced actual cash
value policy that would pay for just what you lost.

In deciding which kind of coverage to buy, there's always
"a trade-off between the price of the insurance and the
amount you recover," says Mooney. You'll pay 10 to 20 percent more for replacement cost policies than for those that
only pay actual cash value. Which you buy will depend on
your business goals and the age and condition of the property
you're covering.

Let's say a business owns the building where it operates,
but the facility is old, in bad condition, and located in an
undesirable part of town. Rather than insure for replacement
cost, it makes more sense to get actual cash value, which
would cover the company's equity in the building, Mooney
says. Likewise, a company that owns offices in a newer building in a good neighborhood would probably prefer a policy
that covers replacement cost.

WHAT DOES IT MEAN TO "SELF-INSURE"?

 A COMPANY THAT GOES THIS ROUTE SETS ASIDE
money to cover potential losses and thinks of that
fund as a substitute for insurance. But the concept
is more applicable to a giant corporation than to a small
operation, says Mooney. As a practical matter, one big
claim could destroy a small business, so most can't afford
to self-insure.

Rather than "going bare" (industry lingo for not buying

insurance), Mooney recommends companies "transfer" the risk—if not by insurance, in some other way. For example, if you employ drivers and are worried about steep premiums for workers' compensation, consider using a common carrier instead. By leasing or renting your work space, rather than owning the building, you transfer the risk of losing that property.

CHAPTER 2

Protecting Innovation and Inventions

FOR MANY COMPANIES, THE MOST VALUABLE thing they own isn't plant and equipment. It's their "intellectual property." That's legal lingo for the bundle of rights that go with products, services, information, and even certain business names.

This complex area of the law covers everything from the words to a song to a secret formula for toothpaste. When something is your intellectual property, you generally have the right to use it yourself, sell it, or license others to use it *(see Q22)*, and stop people from exploiting it without your permission *(see Q32)*.

The key laws to know about are federal statutes covering copyrights, patents, and trademarks. Copyright law deals with art and written work. Patents involve inventions that are new, useful, and "unobvious" (there hasn't been anything like them before). Trademarks apply to words, phrases,

symbols, or devices that identify your goods or
services and distinguish them from those of others.

Trade secrets, the other branch of intellectual
property, protect confidential information that could
give your competitors an edge. Though trade secrets
were traditionally a matter of state law, a 1996
federal statute (the Economic Espionage Act)
imposes stiff criminal penalties for intentionally
taking, receiving, or copying trade secrets without
the owner's permission.

Without delving into all the fine points (which
could take volumes), it's important for you to know
what kinds of things are intellectual property and act
swiftly to protect your rights. Registering your
rights—by getting a copyright, patent, or
trademark—helps secure potentially lucrative
business. It also gives you important protections if
others accuse you of infringement.

Copyrights

STRICTLY A MATTER OF FEDERAL LAW, A COPYRIGHT PROTECTS
an original artistic or literary work, whether or not it's published. Examples of items that can be copyrighted are music,
visual arts, architecture, choreography, and moving pictures.
Whoever holds the copyright can reproduce the material, distribute it, display it, prepare related materials, and (where
relevant) perform it publicly. You can't copyright an idea, but
once you've turned that inspiration into something real, protection can last 100 years or more.

HOW DO I PROTECT A COPYRIGHT?

Q 20 TECHNICALLY YOU HAVE AN AUTOMATIC COPY
right as soon as you create the work. For maximum
legal protection, though, you should put your copyright notice on the work and register it with the U.S. Copyright Office, says Jonathan Kirsch, a lawyer with Kirsch &
Mitchell in Los Angeles and the author of *Kirsch's Handbook
of Publishing Law* (Acrobat Books, $21.95). Neither of these
steps is required, but both offer distinct legal advantages.

Using the copyright notice lets people know you own the
copyright and requires very little effort on your part. The best
form of notice is the symbol © plus the word "Copyright,"
the name of the person or company claiming the right, and
the year that the material was first made public.

You don't have to include this notice to claim copyright
protection, but using the notice can give you distinct economic advantages if you wind up suing for copyright
infringement, Kirsch says. If you have the proper copyright
notice on your work, no one can claim to be an "innocent
infringer"—saying that they used your work without realiz-
ing you owned the copyright. That could increase the damages you collect in a lawsuit.

Before you can bring such a case, though, you must register the copyright. And the sooner the better: unless the work
is registered, either at the time of the infringement or three
months after you "publish" it (distribute copies or offer the
work to others so they can distribute it), you can't recover

attorney's fees, nor can you get what are called "statutory damages" under the copyright law.

The *attorney's fees* section of the law gives you the right to have the other side pay your lawyer if you win a copyright case. Since your lawyer's bill could easily be larger than any damages you collect, this is an important benefit of registration. Without attorney's fees, it might not even make economic sense to sue for copyright infringement.

Having a crack at *statutory damages* is another potential benefit of registration. These damages are designed to punish the wrongdoer, rather than to compensate the victim: you can collect a sum of money (the judge decides how much, from within a range set by law) without showing the infringement actually hurt you financially (something that's often difficult to prove). Statutory damages aren't based on the number of copies but are awarded per "act of infringement" (like printing a book or pirating a video). They range dramatically from $200 per act for unintentional infringements to $100,000 per act for intentional ("willful") infringement.

The law requires that you choose between statutory damages and proving actual harm—you can't do both. However, since actual damages (for example, in the form of your lost profits or the infringer's wrongful profits) are so hard to prove, in most cases it's best to go the statutory damages route, Kirsch says. Often the damages are more than you would get if you were able to show actual harm.

Registering a copyright is much easier than registering other forms of intellectual property and costs very little. Here are the steps to take:

◆ Get the appropriate form for the type of work you want to register, whether it's a sound recording, nondramatic literary work, photograph, or piece of visual art. Call the Copyright Office at 202-707-3000 to find out which form to use. You can get the form directly from them or download it from the agency's Internet site at http://lcweb.loc.gov/copyright.

◆ Complete the form. Follow the instructions on the form or get a lawyer to help you the first time. After that, you can easily do the paperwork yourself.

◆ Mail the form to the Copyright Office, together with copies of the work (the form will tell you how many) and the required filing fee (between $10 and $40, depending on the type of work you're registering). The registration is effective on the day the office receives it, though you may not get a formal receipt for several weeks or even months.

HOW DO I GET THE RIGHT TO USE SOMEONE ELSE'S WORK?

ORDINARILY, CREATIVE PROFESSIONALS—LIKE designers, writers, photographers, and architects— retain the copyright of whatever they produce. That means if someone is creating work for you or has already done something that you want to use, you must get permission.

You can acquire (and the creator can give away) many types of rights, from a "license" to use the work for a specific purpose within a particular time *(see Q22)* (leaving the creator with all other rights) to an "assignment" of the copyright (in which case the creator gives up any claims of ownership). You have greatest flexibility with the second option. Acquiring all rights frees you to reproduce the work or make any future use of it without paying the creator anything more.

With employees, you automatically acquire the copyright for anything an individual creates or invents within the scope of his or her employment. If a staffer's work winds up earning your company a lot of money, the employee is not entitled to anything extra.

Daniel T. Brooks, a lawyer with Cadwalader, Wickersham & Taft in Washington, D.C., recommends getting employees to sign a written agreement assigning both the copyright and the right to patent anything created on your time. Sometimes it's even reasonable to have that assignment extend several months after people leave the company. That way you cover creations which might have been percolating before an employee left.

When dealing with "independent contractors"—people who are not your employees *(see Q54)*—it's essential to specify in writing whatever rights you're acquiring, says Brooks. Otherwise, the work "will typically belong to them—to the exclusion of your rights."

Ideally, you should have the copyright owner assign you all rights before the work is completed. Without such an agreement, a company that has commissioned a computer program, for example, may not have the right to modify it without the programmer's consent.

If the copyright owner won't assign all rights (as most independent contractors won't), it's still best to negotiate the broadest possible grant. Make a list of the various ways you think you might want to use the work (now and in the future), and have a lawyer draw up an agreement that will cover the bases.

In the process of negotiating for rights, you may discover the creator has fewer rights than you thought. Dennis Martin, an attorney with Blakely Skoloff Taylor & Zafman in Los Angeles, gives the example of someone who writes software programs. Often, one program builds upon previous work, which the original author has licensed *(see Q22)* to another party. If you commission someone to tailor the software for a specific purpose, the "author" you're working with "can only convey the copyright in his or her modifications—not the copyright in the underlying work," Martin says. If this author hasn't gotten the necessary permissions, you could "unknowingly be an infringer."

WHAT RIGHTS SHOULD I SELL IN MY OWN WORK?

THIS IS ONE OF THE FEW TIMES WHEN THE LESS you say in writing, the better. That's because the copyright law is very protective of creative people. For freelancers or independent contractors, the transfer of rights must be done in a written contract. The fewer rights you give away, the greater the chances to negotiate additional compensation for other uses of your work.

While the party buying your work has an incentive to spell things out, you're probably better off with something much more bare-bones—especially if you're selling just a limited use of your work. A letter agreement confirming what work is to be done and what you'll be paid is often enough.

Contracts drafted by the party buying those rights typically go much further. Sometimes—though not always—such agreements use the magic words "work for hire" or ask for an assignment of "all rights."

If you sign a contract that contains such broad wording, you give up your copyright, including the right to reproduce the material or to make any future use of it yourself. What's more, the client may alter the work without your permission—or even your knowledge.

When you think you might want to use, adapt, or modify your creation (say you're a writer, artist, musician, or software developer), be careful what you assign, Martin warns. Give away too much, and you could someday find yourself in the awkward (and frustrating) position of being accused of infringing your own work.

A better option for many creative people is some kind of license. This gives the party buying specified rights in your work (the "licensee") the right to exploit those rights for a specific purpose in exchange for a royalty. You retain the copyright and, therefore, the right to use your work for other purposes.

Depending on your bargaining power, you can carve up the rights any way you like. For instance, you can limit the period (or geographic area) to which the license applies. Or you can grant a series of exclusive licenses for individual businesses to use your work for the single purposes that you specify. Sometimes the licensee is willing to accept a non-exclusive grant of rights, leaving you free to make the same grant to other parties.

TIP: Freelancers are better off without a work-for-hire agreement, so that they can negotiate additional compensation if their work is reused.

TIP: One way to avoid all-rights contracts is not to agree to anything labeled "work for hire." But since other factors may be relevant (whether the creative person or the company proposed the project, for example), it's best to check with a lawyer before signing.

Patents

THERE ARE THREE TYPES OF PATENTS, WHICH YOU CAN APPLY
for through the U.S. Patent and Trademark Office.

Utility patents are what most people think of when they
hear the word "patent," and most patents fall into this category. It covers machines, manufactured items, processes,
and "compositions of matter" (like toothpaste, drugs, and
biotechnology products). New uses for old items or processes
are also patentable.

Design patents apply to the unique appearance or decoration of an item (not the structure or how it operates). Sometimes you'll want to apply for both a utility and a design
patent. For instance, the Patent Office notes, if you invent a
self-watering flowerpot, you might get a utility patent on the
mechanism. The floral decoration on the outside of the pot
would be covered by a design patent.

Plant patents are for new varieties of plants that can be
asexually reproduced.

With rare exceptions, a patent lasts 20 years from the date
you file a patent application and can't be renewed. Once the
patent expires, you're free to continue making, using, or selling the item, but you can't stop others from doing the same.

WHAT SHOULD I DO BEFORE APPLYING FOR A PATENT?

THOUGH NOT LEGALLY REQUIRED, A PATENTABIL-
ity search should be your first move, says Joseph
DeGrandi, a patent lawyer with Beveridge,
DeGrandi, Weilacher & Young in Washington, D.C. The
goal is to find out if anybody has come up with an identical
article or "composition"—or something so close to what
you've conceived that the item could have been obvious to
someone in your field. If so, your invention can't be patented,
and you can save yourself the trouble and expense of filing
a patent application. Should you find something that's only
similar to your invention, you still may be able to get a
patent; to do that, though, you'd have to show, on the
claims section of your application *(see Q24)*, how your

invention is different from what's already out there.

The best place to do the patentability search is in the Patent Search Room at the Patent and Trademark Office in Arlington, Virginia. Staff there can direct you to the relevant indexes and give you copies of any patents ($3 apiece) of items similar to yours.

Patents are arranged by class and subclass. For instance, let's say you've invented a particular type of umbrella and want to see if it's patentable. First you'd look in the index under "umbrellas" to find out what class it's in. Then you'd check the index again under headings for the umbrella's particular structure and features (such as handles, ribs, and the open-and-shut mechanism). That will tell you the subclass. If the identical umbrella already exists, you can't patent it.

If, after the patentability search, you're still not sure whether you can patent the item, you may want a patent lawyer to interpret the search results. You can pay the lawyer by the hour for this service (about $150 to $300). A one-hour consultation might help you decide whether to devote any more money and effort to a patent application.

TIP: You can hire a professional to do a patentability search. The searcher will identify the patents that seem most pertinent and mail them to you (about $500 to $1,000). Patent searchers are listed in the Washington, D.C., Yellow Pages (which may be available at your local library). Many are retired patent examiners. It's not necessary that the searcher be a lawyer, but there's no licensing for lay searchers. As with any professional, you'll want to check qualifications. Ask about technical background and years of experience and get names of former clients.

WHAT IS INVOLVED IN GETTING A PATENT?

 FIRST, ACT QUICKLY. YOU MUST FILE AN APPLI-cation within one year of when you first use or sell the invention or tell someone about it, but there are distinct legal advantages to filing even sooner *(see Q25)*.

To have a lawyer or patent "agent" (a nonlawyer who is licensed by the Patent Office to prepare patent applications but is not allowed to appear in court) do a patentability search *(see Q23)* and prepare the application could run $3,000 to $6,000 on the low end to $10,000 or $12,000 for complex inventions (like medical devices, drugs, or chemical compositions). The more you do yourself, the less it costs.

The application consists of many parts, including a detailed description of the invention, drawings, and what's called the "claims" section. This last part of the application, by far the most important and time-consuming to prepare, must point out at least one unique feature of the invention. How well you complete this section could determine whether or not you get the patent. And, if you later bring a patent infringement lawsuit, it could make or break the case.

Once you've submitted the application, along with the appropriate filing fee (a small business would pay $385 for a utility patent, $160 for a design patent, and $265 for a plant patent), the patent office will respond with a letter (called an "office action") telling you whether you can get a patent. Sometimes there's considerable back and forth as you try to convince the examiner that your invention is patentable. It typically takes about two years after you file the application to get the patent, but the process can drag on much longer for complicated inventions.

When you get the patent, there are additional charges. You must pay a "patent issue fee" when you get the patent and various "maintenance" charges during the life of the patent. For a small business, these extra charges would total $3,720 for a utility patent, $3,295 for a design patent, and $3,400 for a plant patent.

If you can't afford this complex and costly route or your invention isn't very valuable to begin with, you might get some protection for manufacturing processes by treating them as trade secrets and taking steps to protect them *(see Q30–31)*, says Herbert Wamsley, a lawyer and executive director of the Intellectual Property Owners Association in Washington, D.C. The risk, of course, is that if your processes become public for more than a year, you may lose your ability to get a patent. Nor will this strategy work as well for products as it might for processes: once you bring products to market, they'll be available for all to see—and copy.

TIP: When products similar to your invention already exist, an experienced professional can work wonders in the claims section. To save money, you could prepare a draft yourself and ask a lawyer to review it. Or go it alone and hope a kindly patent examiner will point you in the right direction if need be. Officially, the patent office doesn't offer such assistance, but Joseph DeGrandi says he's occasionally seen patent examiners help inventors with the claims section of the application.

FYI: *Patent Attorneys and Agents Registered to Practice Before the U.S. Patent and Trademark Office*, published by the Patent and Trademark Office and available for $31 from 202-512-1800, is a directory of about 17,000 professionals arranged alphabetically and geographically. The office won't vouch for any of the people listed, but the book is one starting point in finding professional help with your patent application. If you don't want to purchase the volume, you can access it on the Patent and Trademark Office Internet site (http://www.uspto.gov).

WHO GETS THE PATENT IF TWO PEOPLE INVENT THE SAME THING AT ONCE?

 SINCE PENDING PATENT APPLICATIONS ARE kept secret, it often happens that two people file an application for the same invention. The good news is that under U.S. law, the first person to invent the item gets the patent. To determine who that is, an examiner who discovers the duplicate patent applications will declare what's called an "interference." This proceeding, held before the Board of Patent Appeals and Interferences, gives each side a chance to prove that they were the first to conceive of the invention and put it into practice.

If you filed your application first, that can help your case: the law presumes that you were the earlier inventor unless the other side can prove you wrong. In the United States, whoever proves that he or she was the first inventor wins the interference. Because of the complexity of this courtlike proceeding, it's best to have a patent lawyer represent you during the interference (lawyers' fees: $2,000 to $5,000).

The date of filing is even more important if you want to get a patent in a foreign country, DeGrandi says. You must file a separate patent application in foreign countries in order to get protection there (other countries don't honor U.S. patents). And outside the United States, the first to file usually gets the patent. But most countries will give you the benefit of an earlier application date if you filed for a U.S. patent first.

Before lawyers get too deeply into the proceeding, however, they will probably try to settle with the other side, DeGrandi says. One way to do this is by agreeing in advance that whoever gets the patent will license the other party to use the product or process (see Q22).

Occasionally, patent applications—or even issued patents—fall through the cracks, and the patent office winds up granting two patents for the same item. When that happens, the parties must fight it out (typically in court, but sometimes through the patent office) to determine who was the first inventor. Often the parties work out a licensing agreement (see Q22).

CAN I PROTECT A PRODUCT FROM COPYCATS BEFORE I MARKET IT?

 YOU SHOULD CONSIDER THE FOLLOWING measures:

1 **File a patent application as soon as you can.** An early filing date will help you in an interference proceeding (see Q25), and if you want to market overseas (see Q25).

2 **File a provisional patent application.** You have this option with a utility or a plant patent (but not for a design patent). The provisional patent application is simpler to prepare and has a lower filing fee ($75 for a small business) than the final application. Assuming it includes all necessary information and you file the final application within a year, you get credit for the earlier filing date if there's any dispute about who invented something first (see Q25).

3 Mark your product "patent pending," or "patent applied for" as soon as you've sent in the application. Using these terms offers no legal protection but serves a practical purpose: it discourages competitors from knocking off your product while you're awaiting a patent. Put this notice on the item and the package, giving it the maximum visibility you can without ruining aesthetics, advises Tom Arnold, a patent attorney with Arnold, White & Durkee in Houston. (You're not required to use these terms, but if you do, you must already have a standard or provisional patent application on file. Otherwise, you might be subject to a fine.) Once you get the patent, you'll want to switch the legend to read "Patent," "pat.," or "U.S. patent" and include the patent number.

4 Do an infringement search before you spend a substantial sum on the manufacturing, marketing, or advertising of anything new. Here you're looking at whether the claims of any issued patent *(see Q24)* cover the product or process you want to put on the market. The key is to avoid surprise lawsuits once you've brought your product to market.

Just like the patentability search *(see Q23)*, the infringement search starts with the patent office indexes. Only this time, you'll also want to read the patents already issued for items like yours. Having this search done by a professional patent searcher costs about $3,000 at the low end and can run $15,000 or more if your invention is complex or you need to search internationally.

Trademarks

WHILE A PATENT PROTECTS YOUR PRODUCT, A TRADEMARK covers the name or logo you give to it. A service mark is the same as a trademark except that it applies to services rather than goods.

Once you've registered your trademark or service mark (the application is the same), it lasts for an initial 10 years, but you can renew it indefinitely as long as you continue to use the mark to identify your goods or services.

HOW CAN I REDUCE THE COST OF REGISTERING A TRADEMARK?

Q 27 HIRING A LAWYER TO HANDLE THE ENTIRE procedure could wind up costing $1,000 to $5,000 or more. But you needn't turn the whole job over to an attorney. You can slash the bill by as much as 90 percent by doing some of the work yourself and with the help of professional trademark search firms. Here's how:

◆ **Check to see whether the name or symbol you want is already registered.** You can do this by visiting one of the 78 Patent and Trademark Depository Libraries, usually located at public libraries and universities around the country. (Call 703-308-HELP to find the one nearest you.) You can look up trademarks in book form or, for more up-to-date information, on CD-ROMs. Be sure to check words that sound similar but are spelled differently—like "dog" and "dawg" or "cheese" and "cheez." Then consult the *Official Gazette*, a weekly paperback update of trademarks and applications pending, which you can also find at the Patent and Trademark Depository Library.

You can also tap directly into the Federal Trademark Registry via the on-line Trademarkscan database on the computer network CompuServe (cost: $4.80 per hour plus $20 to search up to five trademarks). If you don't want to spend time checking the registry yourself and don't mind paying some bucks, hire a trademark search service such as Thomson & Thomson at 800-692-8833 (typical cost: $80 to $330 per search). A lawyer can order the search for you, and if the firm gets a volume discount (as many do) you may spend no more than you would pay to order the search directly. And then you can get the lawyer to analyze the search results, which is the most important part.

TIP: Ask lawyers whether they mark up the cost of searches ordered from a search firm. A lawyer should be willing to tailor an approach to your business and budget.

FYI: A common misconception is that incorporating your business provides trademark protection. It doesn't.

- **Do a common-law search.** Names or marks that are in use may be protected even though they've never been registered. So the next step is to search for such names, a task complicated enough that it's best given to a professional search service. Thomson & Thomson, for example, owns an extensive proprietary database designed specifically to locate common-law trademarks (cost: $175).

- **Consult a lawyer to review your findings.** Only a trademark attorney can tell you whether the names you turned up resemble too closely those you want to use (typical cost: $300 to $600 and up).

- **File registration papers.** Call the Trademark Assistance Center at 703-308-9000 for its free 31-page pamphlet, *Basic Facts About Trademarks*, which includes the application and instructions for completing it.

TIP: If you want to economize further, you can take these steps in stages. For example, during the start-up phase, you can do the preliminary search yourself and file an application. Once you know you have a winning concept you can order a more thorough search and get a legal opinion.

FYI: *Trademark: Legal Care for Your Business & Product Name,* by Kate McGrath and Stephen Elias (Nolo Press, $29.95), is a complete primer on trademarks, written in plain English. Chapter 8 takes you through the trademark registration process step-by-step.

CAN I TRADEMARK AN INTERNET DOMAIN NAME?

YES, BUT THE TRADEMARK OFFICE DOESN'T assign Internet addresses, says David Bender, an attorney with White & Case in New York City.

Right now, that process is administered by Network Solutions, Inc., a Reston, Virginia, company that assigns, records, and tracks domain names in the United States, and there may soon be other players in the market. Although the company's rules are in flux, so far, the person who gets to them first usually has the right to use a domain name. (The latest rules are posted on the company's Website at http://rs.internic.net.)

On the whole, Network Solutions doesn't get in the middle of domain name disputes. One exception is that if you've trademarked a name or used it before the company approved someone else's domain name. In that case, you can invoke a complex procedure for temporarily getting the address put on "hold," until a court decides who's entitled to it. On the other hand, if you have the domain name and it turns out someone else trademarked it first, you risk losing your Internet address.

Before you invest time and money in applying for a domain name, do a trademark search *(see Q27)* to see whether the name is already associated with another business, Bender advises. If it is, you'll need to find a different Internet address.

CAN I TRADEMARK A VANITY PHONE NUMBER?

YOU CAN'T TRADEMARK THE NUMBER, BUT YOU can trademark the name it spells (such as 1-800-GO-U-HAUL) and, assuming it's available as a phone number, turn it into yours, says Daniel T. Brooks. If telemarketing will be an important part of your venture, Brooks suggests you simultaneously apply for the number and register your trademark.

Still, getting trademark protection probably won't stop another company from copying your idea in a different area code, says Brooks. For example, if your number is 1-800-PIRATES, someone else would be free to use 1-703-PIRATES. The recent addition of new toll-free exchanges leaves open the possibility that more than one business in the toll-free market will adopt almost the same vanity number.

Trade Secrets

BEHIND MOST TRADE SECRET PROTECTIONS ARE TWO ASSUMPtions. The first is that you have valuable information not generally known to others—everything from customer lists and business methods to special formulas and knowledge of the company's pricing structure. The second is that this information has leaked out despite your best efforts to guard it. There's no procedure for registering trade secrets, so it's important you take precautions to keep the material secret *(see Q30–31)*. Trade secrets can last forever, as long as they're not discovered.

HOW CAN I STOP EMPLOYEES FROM COMPETING WITH MY BUSINESS IF THEY LEAVE THE COMPANY?

 THESE KINDS OF TRADE SECRETS PROBLEMS often come up when workers move from one company to another.

Documenting your concerns and asking staff to agree to them in writing gives you a basis for taking legal action if problems later arise. James H.A. Pooley, an attorney with Fish & Richardson in Menlo Park, California, recommends you consider the following terms:

◆ **Confidentiality agreement.** Clearly define what's a trade secret and require that every employee agree not to disclose this confidential material.

◆ **Nonsolicitation agreement.** Where appropriate, specify that staff who leave your company won't solicit customers (or other employees).

◆ **Assignment of inventions.** For employees above the clerical level who work in creative positions, get an agreement that your company owns anything they invent as part of their employment.

◆ **Noncompete agreement.** This is a promise not to join a rival company for a set time after leaving your work force. While they can avoid messy fights over what's a trade secret, noncompete agreements are also highly controversial. Laws vary dramatically from state to state. California prohibits these agreements unless they're necessary to protect confidential information, like customer lists. Elsewhere, courts and legislatures have required that contracts be "reasonable" in terms of how long they last and what territory they apply to and protect a legitimate employer interest (such as confidential information).

Courts have spilled a lot of ink applying these standards. A "reasonable" time span is typically a year or two. The narrower a geographic restriction is, the more likely it will survive attack. For example, salespeople may be restrained from working in their previous territory.

When asking current employees to sign a non-compete agreement, it's best to offer extra cash, stock options, or other perks. Some courts have said this is required. You can have workers sign before they're hired or at the time of a promotion or large bonus.

You'll want to remind employees of the noncompete agreement when they leave the company—for whatever reason. When you fire a worker or a staffer resigns, reiterate the obligation not to disclose trade secrets. Collect any confidential material you've given them. Indicate that if any problems arise, the company is going to enforce its rights.

TIP: When recruiting new staff, find out whether people you're about to hire signed a noncompete agreement at the prior job. Even if they haven't, Pooley suggests you ask for a written agreement that they won't take private information (like knowledge of the company's products and prices) from the prior job and use it at your company. If they do and the previous employer sues you, these assurances would provide some protection: you could argue that your company was innocent—that the misappropriation came from a rogue employee who leaked information despite your best efforts to avoid it.

HOW CAN I PREVENT A TRADE SECRET FROM LEAKING OUT TO NONEMPLOYEES?

Q 31 SOME RELATIONSHIPS, SUCH AS THOSE WITH lawyers, accountants, bankers, and financial advisers, are by nature confidential; these professionals should know not to leak secrets. Other times you can't make that assumption. In these cases, notify the person you're dealing with that information you share is confidential, get a written agreement when possible, and "be sure your own behavior is consistent with any expectations you've expressed orally or in writing," Pooley advises.

◆ **Confidentiality agreements.** Often it's enough to say, "This is just between us, okay?" or "Can you keep a secret?" before sharing one. You should also prominently mark materials (like the business plans you submit to venture capitalists) "confidential." Receiving the information then implies an obligation on the person's part to protect the material. But it's even better to confirm your understanding in writing.

This is particularly true when dealing with independent contractors—sometimes called consultants or freelancers (see Q54). Whether you retain them to conduct market research or to review your benefits plan, one thing that makes these independents valuable is their industry savvy. Yet the competing loyalties that consultants face raises the possibility that your secrets will leak out—if not intentionally, inadvertently. Having a written agreement sensitizes everyone to the issues.

In some relationships, the parties routinely communicate in writing, and there's ample opportunity to slip in a warning about confidentiality without sending a separate document. For instance, you could include such a notice on the forms you send to customers or mechanical drawings submitted to vendors. ("This is confidential to ABC company. It can only be used to fulfill the order.")

TIP: When, for one reason or another, you can't get a written confidentiality agreement, Pooley recommends you create what's called an "estoppel by silence." To do that, you might send a letter that says something like, "It was very good to meet with you. I'm looking forward to discussing the details of this project next week. Our conversations are, of course, confidential." A notice like that, followed by the recipient's silence, legally bars the person from later arguing that there was no confidentiality, Pooley says.

◆ **Follow-up.** Once you've told people that material is proprietary, don't drop the subject, Pooley advises. Point out any behavior inconsistent with the terms of confidentiality agreements. Reinforce obligations through additional letters and forms, stamps of "confidential" on any new drafts of material, and reminders when you set up meetings that the subjects discussed will be confidential.

◆ **Corporate security.** To guard against corporate thieves, you'll also want to be sure your physical plant and computer system are secure. Sample precautions: screen visitors, issue passwords, and lock areas (like desks, file cabinets, or rooms) where you store trade secrets.

Having an Internet site creates other potential leaks. With the touch of a button, one of your own workers might inadvertently post sensitive material (like new products plans) for the whole world to see. Unless you install high-tech protections, outsiders who sign on to look at your home page could theoretically go much further, accessing confidential documents. If you're concerned about any of these possibilities, consult one of the growing number of computer security experts. Local computer users' groups can help you find a reputable one in your area.

Asserting Your Rights

IT CAN BE MADDENING TO FIND OUT THAT OTHERS ARE profiting from your intellectual property. But it's best to cool off and find the most practical way to address the problem.

61

CAN I PREVENT COMPETITORS FROM COPYING MY NEW SERVICE IDEA?

SINCE U.S. LAW FAVORS COMPETITION, SERVICE ideas generally can't be protected once they become public. However, rules on safeguarding intellectual property can offer you some protection. For instance, you may be able to copyright *(see Q20)* your marketing materials and get a service mark *(see introduction to Q27)* for the name, logo, or advertising slogan you choose for the new service.

If you think you have common-law rights *(see Q27)*, in the name, logo, or slogan, use the symbol "SM" on any printed material about the service. This gives other people notice of your stake and might deter them from copying it.

Once you've registered the mark, you would use the symbol ® (or mark the materials "Registered U.S. Patent and

Trademark Office," abbreviated "Reg. U.S. Pat. & Tm. Off.") to accomplish the same purpose. Another option is to say the same thing in plain English: "[Name Your Service] is a registered service mark of XYZ Corporation."

TIP: It's not necessary for you to have actually started offering goods or services in order to apply for a trademark or service mark. You just indicate on the standard trademark or service mark application the date on which you plan to start using your mark. This operates as an "intent-to-use" application and protects you while you're starting up. However, the registration process won't be complete until you actually begin using the mark and submit some additional paperwork. This is either a "Statement of Use," if the Patent and Trademark Office has already approved your intent-to-use application, or an "Amendment to Allege Use," if it hasn't. You would use the same form for both: PTO Form 1553, "Allegation of Use for Intent-to-Use Applications, with Declaration," available from the Patent and Trademark Office, or on the agency's Web site.

TIP: In addition, during the planning stages, you can further safeguard your service idea by limiting the number of employees and outside parties you disclose it to and by having them sign confidentiality agreements *(see Q30)*. Stamp relevant documents "confidential proprietary information," restrict access to file cabinets where they are stored, and whatever you do, don't toss your drafts in the office recycling bin. Circulate as few copies as possible and require venture capitalists or other outside parties to sign a written agreement that they will not divulge your secret or use it for their personal advantage *(see Q31)*.

WHAT CAN I DO IF A MUCH LARGER BUSINESS INFRINGES MY PATENT, COPYRIGHT, OR TRADEMARK?

 YOUR FIRST INCLINATION IS PROBABLY TO "SUE the bastards," and on the surface, the law provides you with some attractive remedies. For instance, in a copyright infringement case, you can get statutory damages *(see Q20)*, and a court may order that the infringing work be seized and destroyed. In a trademark case, the court could impose stiff penalties, order the infringer to change its name or mark, or even require that it throw away products.

When interstate commerce is involved (which is almost always) and you suspect someone of intentionally taking, receiving, or copying your trade secrets without permission, federal criminal law kicks in. Penalties could include lengthy jail terms and substantial fines. Obviously, the government—not your company—gets the fines, but the prospect of criminal sanctions certainly strengthens your hand.

Except in the last instance, when the U.S. Attorney's office would handle the case (that is, assuming they want to prosecute), you must foot the legal bill and spend valuable time in litigation, rather than running your business. How bad can it get? A typical patent infringement suit, which could take five years to wind its way through trial and appeal, often runs up $1 million in legal fees, says patent attorney Tom Arnold. Big cases can take much longer and cost even more.

Nor are the winners and losers always clearly defined. With patents, perhaps the haziest branch of intellectual property law, the standards on the validity and scope of patents "are the most vague and indefinite that exist anywhere in jurisprudence," says Arnold. Similarly, when someone rips off a copyrighted work but makes minor changes, it's up to the judge or jury to decide whether the two works are "substantially similar." Here, too, there can be considerable wrangling.

Although a large company may be able to shoulder huge litigation expenses, even the Goliaths of this world are looking to rein in legal fees. Do see a lawyer as soon as you spot the infringement. But also be aware that there are options short of a lawsuit. Without compromising any rights, you may be able to solve the problem outside the courthouse.

For patent, copyright, or trademark infringement, the first step is a "cease and desist" letter. As its formal name implies, this correspondence (most powerful if it comes on a lawyer's letterhead) demands that the infringer stop. Sometimes recipients bristle, hire a lawyer, and put up their own fight. More often, such a letter is enough to scare them into compliance.

With misappropriation of trade secrets, it may be enough to confront the party who leaked the secret and the party that person told, James Pooley says. Often, you get them to promise not to use the information or to tell anyone else.

TIP: Other popular compromises for intellectual property disputes include negotiating licenses *(see Q22)*, royalties, shared rights in the protected material, or agreements to get out of the business. For patents, there's the possibility of what are called "design arounds"—where the party accused of infringement stops making the exact patented feature; in exchange for producing a slightly less competitive item, that company gets a concession that the product doesn't infringe.

TIP: If negotiations fail, you don't necessarily have to litigate. Before or after filing a suit there's the possibility of ending the conflict swiftly (and economically) through so-called alternative dispute resolution methods, such as mediation and arbitration *(see Q97)*.

WHAT SHOULD I DO IF ONE OF THE GIANTS ACCUSES ME OF COPYRIGHT, TRADEMARK, OR PATENT INFRINGEMENT, OR MISAPPROPRIATING TRADE SECRETS?

WHEN A SMALL COMPANY LOSES SUCH A CASE, IT could be out of business. Even before then, you have the practical problem of how you'll pay a lawyer to defend you.

The second hurdle may be surmountable in a copyright case. Whether they're plaintiffs or defendants in an infringement case, owners of registered works *(see Q20)* can get attorneys' fees if they win. That could make it easier to find a lawyer to defend you. Beware, though: how much you get in attorneys' fees is up to the court; if you are awarded less than you owe the lawyer, you could get stuck paying the difference.

Still, whether you win or lose, it's tough to litigate against someone who can afford hefty legal bills. Which is one reason why it's so important for small businesses to seek out-of-court options *(see Chapter 7)*.

Arnold suggests you begin with a conciliatory response to the "cease and desist" letter *(see Q33)*. For instance, in a patent case, you (or your lawyer) might say something like: "We are the kind of people who honor patents. In exchange, we ask you to honor appropriate design-around efforts *(see Q33)*. Let's meet and explore possible solutions short of courthouse warfare."

Jonathan Kirsch, of Kirsch & Mitchell, also offers a ray of hope. Often when a big corporation goes after a smaller one because they think it's infringing, the primary motive is to get a product off the market, he says. In those cases, all the small business needs to do is offer to stop. Sometimes the larger entity that sued is even willing to pay some money to make that possible.

For instance, if you need to redesign your signs, stationery, and uniforms to steer clear of a larger company's trademark infringement claim, you might get their help financing those changes. In a copyright infringement case, the larger company might be willing to let you sell off your existing inventory of the material they object to.

Such settlements may not seem very satisfying at first—especially if you think you're in the right. But they can save you a bundle in legal fees and eliminate the risk of a giant judgment.

CHAPTER 3

Finding Affordable, Quality Legal Advice

T HERE'S SOMETHING ALIEN——AND ALIENATING——
about the way lawyers operate. They talk in lingo
that's tough to understand. They're among the few
professionals who routinely charge for their time by
the hour. And as if the price of these services
weren't high enough, they bill for costs that most
other businesses treat as overhead—photocopies,
faxes, and long-distance phone calls, for instance.

The lawyer-client relationship can be very
intense, particularly when the stakes are high.
Ideally, you should be able to trust this professional.
But with most billing structures, there's a built-in
tension. Clients want to get matters resolved swiftly,
early on, and keep the bill down. Lawyers have every
incentive to maximize their profits.

Some large businesses have lawyers to manage
the lawyers. Typically, they're staff attorneys who
handle some of the company's legal work

themselves and oversee any outside experts. Other times, a business hires an independent auditor to review its legal bills and look for fat.

Most small businesses can't afford this extra layer of supervision. Their best defense against legal sticker shock is to become smart consumers. That means choosing the best person for a given task, negotiating a fee arrangement that's good for both sides, and not paying for any unnecessary services or expenses. Many good lawyers are hungry for business. That gives clients considerable bargaining power.

Hiring a Lawyer

CHANCES ARE, YOU WOULDN'T BUY A CAR WITHOUT A test drive. Yet many companies hire lawyers with little regard for the professional's qualifications, personal style, or even fees. Some business owners wind up regretting the hasty choice.

HOW DO I SHOP FOR A LAWYER?

 THE IDEAL TIME TO LOOK FOR A LAWYER IS before you really need one. Here are some steps to take:

◆ **Ask for referrals.** The best ones come from business owners who've been involved in similar cases or from people whose judgment you trust—like bankers, financial advisers, or other lawyers. State and local bar associations can direct you to attorneys in your area but can't vouch for their skills.

Referrals from trade associations can also be a good bet since, at least in theory, someone else has already done the legwork to find lawyers sensitive to your needs. That doesn't mean you should suspend all judgment, but it's a start.

FYI: The most complete source of lawyers' names is the *Martindale-Hubbell Law Directory*, which lists attorneys by state and by area of practice. It is available in many public libraries, and on the Internet at http://www.martindale.com.

◆ **Interview at least two lawyers before you choose one.** Your initial conversation can take place by phone, but it's a good idea to meet in person before you agree to work together. To avoid surprises, ask whether you'll have to pay for these preliminary talks. (Sample wording: "I'm trying to decide which lawyer to hire and would like to spend 15 minutes talking with you. Is there a charge for that time?")

On the phone, briefly inquire about the lawyer's expertise in relevant areas and experience working with small businesses. If you're considering a suit, determine lawyers' openness to less costly and time-consuming alternatives such as arbitration and mediation *(see Q95).*

Save detailed discussion of your case and negotiation of fees *(see Q39)* for later; until the lawyer knows more about your situation, he or she often doesn't have enough information to quote an accurate number.

◆ **At a face-to-face meeting, get more details about a**

lawyer's experience handling other similar cases. Some questions you should ask: What percent of your work involves issues like the ones we're discussing? Can you describe some recent cases, including the results? What are the strong and weak points of my case? How long do you think this matter will take? What nonlegal options might I consider? What are your fees?

◆ **Find out whether this lawyer will handle the entire matter or delegate some portions to a more junior attorney or paralegal (a nonlawyer legal assistant).** Before signing on, ask to meet the other people who will be working on the case. Adding extra staff to your matter increases legal costs geometrically, says John W. Toothman, whose Alexandria, Virginia, consulting firm, The Devil's Advocate, helps companies cut legal costs. You must pay not just for the time they personally bill, but also for the time everyone else bills to talk to them.

◆ **Discuss your goals along with possible legal strategies, and ask for an estimate of what it will cost to handle your case.** Not every dispute must lead to a lawsuit. Of those that do, 90 percent wind up being settled. It's important to know whether your lawyer is a gladiator or a peacemaker. Many good lawyers try to resolve things through letters, phone calls, or in-person negotiations. In such cases you can pay the lawyer by the hour ($150 to $350 is typical) plus expenses (like photocopying) to do what's needed.

◆ **End the interview by getting names of past clients.** You'll want to ask these clients whether the lawyer was honest, listened to what they had to say, promptly returned phone calls, and provided weekly or monthly updates about what was happening. Even an attorney who insists on confidentiality should be able to offer at least a couple of references from past clients.

◆ **Finally, if you're shopping for a trial lawyer, watch the attorney in court before hiring him or her.** Just because people are smart, doesn't mean they know how to try cases.

TIP: How can you find out when—and where—a prospective lawyer is appearing in court? Certainly, you can ask, but independent means are even better. If you hear (or read) about a case the lawyer is handling, you can call the court, ask which judge is hearing the case, and then call that judge's chambers to find out when the next court appearance is scheduled. The day before, confirm the information with the judge's chambers, since court dates sometimes change at the last minute. Most proceedings are open to the public, so you won't need permission to sit in; just ask the courthouse guard which courtroom to go to.

WHICH IS BETTER: ONE ALL-PURPOSE LAWYER OR VARIOUS SPECIALISTS?

Q 36 MANY SMALL BUSINESSES FIND IT'S MOST economical to use a combination of the two. The chief advantage of a good general practitioner is that he or she knows your business and can be available when the queries come. A short call to clear up potential problems could save you a bigger bill later.

This works best when the professional knows his or her limitations and is willing to pass along work (and give up fees) if another lawyer would be better for the task. The trouble is, some attorneys with no expertise in a particular matter are either desperate for business or don't know when to say no. There's a risk then that they'll accept cases they're not qualified to handle.

While a clever, conscientious lawyer could conceivably tackle almost anything, I'd prefer a specialist for most of the subjects covered in this book. A good business lawyer could prepare a basic contract or lease, but you'd want someone with greater expertise to handle cases involving employment law, intellectual property, zoning, and estate planning, for instance. Even if they charge more by the hour, chances are you won't be paying for them to learn about the issues that concern you. If you deal with a general practitioner for everyday issues but want a specialist for anything more involved, be sure your primary lawyer understands that. Knowing there's more than one lawyer in the picture also has the advantage of keeping legal fees competitive.

TIP: Most lawyers charge by the hour for everyday business matters, so beware of anyone who asks you for money in advance or offers to perform specific services for a flat fee *(see Q39)*. Often they are bait-and-switch arrangements or include extras that carry an additional charge.

SHOULD I GO TO A LARGE FIRM OR A SOLE PRACTITIONER?

 ON THE SURFACE, SOLE PRACTITIONERS MAY seem like an economical choice. Their rates tend to be lower than those of lawyers at larger firms. Another attraction is that they're small businesses themselves and may share (or at least understand) your entrepreneurial spirit.

What's key is that any lawyers you choose must have enough experience to address your full range of needs—or the good sense, when they're in over their heads, to refer you to others. Conscientious as a sole practitioner might be, you don't want to pay the lawyer by the hour while he or she gets up to speed.

Most Lone Rangers can't afford the staffing and other resources you'd get with a larger operation. If your matter requires legal research, for instance, the lawyer may "farm it out," take a markup, and charge you as much as you'd pay a larger firm for the same service.

Plus, like everyone else, sole practitioners have pressure to pay the rent. This tempts some of them to ring up unnecessary billable hours if you happen to catch them in a lean month.

With a medium or large-sized firm, you might pay more by the hour but have a lower legal bill in the long run. That could happen when a name-brand lawyer (or firm) has the know-how (or connections) to bring your matter to a quick resolution. Chances are the firm also has standard documents on file and can save you money by not drafting everything from scratch.

Still, the larger the firm, the greater the potential conflicts of interest. These are situations where the firm's representation of another client could interfere with its ability to act in your best interest. Conflicts can be blatant, like representing both parties to a lawsuit, or more subtle. Example: you're negotiating a contract with Big Company X but the firm already represents that business in an unrelated suit against another party.

In the latter case, you might choose to "waive the conflict"—have the firm represent you anyway, since the risks seem so remote. On the other hand, if the firm might have trouble serving two masters, you'd be better off taking your business elsewhere.

If you decide to go with a medium or large firm, consider retaining a senior associate (5 to 10 years' experience) or junior partner (8 to 15 years' experience). These lawyers tend to bill their time at lower rates than senior partners. You also avoid situations where a heavy hitter puts aside (or delegates) your work when a bigger matter comes along.

TIP: If you're dealing with a medium or large-sized firm, consider working with one of the growing number of lawyers called "of counsel." Traditionally, these were retirees or emeritus types, but more and more they include much younger attorneys who don't generate enough business to become equity partners. Either way, lawyers who are of counsel can be a good bet for small-business owners who seek competence at reasonable rates.

IS IT MORE ECONOMICAL TO HAVE A LAWYER ON STAFF OR TO RELY EXCLUSIVELY ON OUTSIDE LAW FIRMS?

Q 38 THE ANSWER DEPENDS ENTIRELY ON THE volume of your legal work and the kind of expertise you typically need. Large companies tend to rely on a combination of the two: for them, in-house lawyers can function as good general practitioners or as specialists who handle matters that arise frequently in a company's work (like patent, trademark, and copyright issues). Compared with the high cost of outside counsel, keeping lawyers on staff at a large company can yield huge savings.

Unless a small company has a steady volume of legal

work and lawyers' bills topping about $300,000 a year, it probably makes more sense to hire lawyers as you need them than to keep one on staff. Here's how you figure: the ideal in-house counsel is an experienced attorney, and salary and fringe benefits for that person could run anywhere from $150,000 to $300,000 a year. You wouldn't save any money until yearly legal expenses exceed that amount. What's more, when complex issues arise, at least some in-house lawyers will need to consult outside firms, adding to your expenses.

HOW SHOULD I NEGOTIATE LEGAL FEES?

 ALTHOUGH MANY PEOPLE ARE HESITANT TO discuss money with a lawyer, it's important to strike a deal that's good for you both. What fee schedule works best varies with the case. These are some common options:

◆ **Hourly fees.** Most lawyers charge by the hour—anything from $150 to $400, depending on the location and size of the firm. Charges are usually broken out in five-, six- or ten-minute increments. You typically pick up expenses like photocopying and faxes *(see Q44)*.

Don't assume that the lawyer who charges the most is the best or be afraid to negotiate hourly rates (some lawyers have different rates for different clients). Also ask about time-keeping increments and whether the lawyer rounds off time to the nearest quarter hour (which could inflate your bill).

◆ **Flat rates.** Some lawyers offer flat rates for routine matters such as drafting a contract, reviewing a lease, or preparing incorporation papers. Flat fees make it easier to compare prices and to negotiate (after getting several quotes, you can ask the lawyer you choose to match the lowest fee, for example). Be aware, however, that a lawyer who charges a flat fee may not be generous with his or her time. For matters handled on a flat fee, you also may be required to pay some money up front and the balance upon completion.

TIP: Each type of fee arrangement has its own incentives. While flat fees make it easier to compare prices, they discourage lawyers from spending extra time on your matter. With hourly rates, on the other hand, the incentive is to run up the meter. Usually, you're better off paying by the hour. But to be sure (and keep those billable hours to a minimum), always get an estimate of how long a particular task will take.

◆ **Retainer fees.** This term has more than one meaning, so don't use it without spelling out your arrangement. A true retainer is a monthly or yearly flat fee for specified services. But it can also mean money paid up front like a deposit.

If your lawyer uses the word "retainer" in this second sense, be sure to clearly establish what it covers. Ideally, it should be applied to expenses and to the lawyer's hourly fee, rather than just used to reserve his or her time. Insist on an agreement that at least some of this advance will be refundable if you fire the lawyer or don't use up the retainer within a set period (say, 60 days).

TIP: Watch out for lawyers who offer you cut rates in exchange for shares in your growing business, John Toothman says. Sometimes they think that entitles them to a say in how you run it. A better option is to pay as you go. If you're just starting up and can't afford that, ask whether your lawyer would postpone billing until you're up and running.

◆ **Contingency fees.** If you're the one bringing a suit (the "plaintiff") in certain kinds of cases, a lawyer might be willing to take the case "on contingency," meaning all or part of the fee is paid out of any settlement or judgment. These arrangements are most common in the context of personal injury cases, but you may be able to negotiate them for certain kinds of business disputes. The most likely candidates are cases for patent, trademark, and copyright infringement if you have a very strong case against a highly solvent defendant.

Straight contingency cases, in which your lawyer gets nothing until the case is resolved, are highly unusual in the business context these days. Far more common are hybrid arrangements in which the client also pays a reduced hourly rate for certain services or picks up expenses such as court filing fees, deposition costs, and payments to expert witnesses.

To protect yourself against any surprises, it's best to set a ceiling on the total tab.

◆ **You also can negotiate the percentage that the lawyer gets, whether it's the standard one-third or less.** The lawyer may agree to a lower percentage if you're willing to pay costs as they're incurred (rather than out of whatever you recover) or if you have an especially strong case.

◆ **Another possibility is to agree to a sliding scale contingency fee, where how much a lawyer takes depends on the stage at which the case gets resolved.** For instance, you might agree that the lawyer will get 20 percent if the matter settles before a court case is filed; 25 percent after the papers are filed but before costly "discovery" (document requests and sworn testimony before trial); 33 percent after discovery but before trial; 40 percent at trial; and 45 percent on appeal.

◆ **No matter how trustworthy (or intimidating) the lawyer seems, get your agreement in writing (some states require it).** It should outline what the fee covers (including paralegal time, long-distance phone calls, and photocopying) and require detailed monthly or quarterly statements that itemize all charges. If you're being billed by the hour, prohibit the lawyer from spending more than a certain number of hours without your prior approval. Should the lawyer disregard your instructions and try to collect more, you'll have a solid defense.

◆ **You'll also want to cover what happens if you switch firms (better to say up front how the fees will be calculated than get into legal tangles later).** In many contingency cases, for instance, the first lawyer still gets part of what you recover. To avoid winding up in court with your lawyer, provide in your agreement that fee disputes will be submitted to arbitration or mediation *(see Q95).*

TIP: When your lawyer is actively involved in a matter, getting billed every 30 days gives you a chance to stop the firm from going off on tangents that wind up costing you more.

TIP: If you're hiring the lawyer to defend you in a suit, you might consider a "reverse" contingency fee, says Kenneth Menendez, an Atlanta lawyer whose consulting company, Legal Solutions, advises businesses about how to reduce legal costs. Here you and the lawyer agree on a benchmark that represents the maximum amount you could get stuck paying. You pay the lawyer at least part of what he or she saves you off this sum.

For example, let's say you're sued for $1 million and you figure at worst you'll have to pay $500,000. If the worst-case scenario comes true, the lawyer gets nothing—saving you a hefty lawyer's bill on top of what you must pay your opponent. If the judgment against you is $400,000 (or you wind up settling for that amount), the lawyer gets some portion of $100,000 ($500,000 minus $400,000).

How much of these savings the lawyer receives is something to negotiate in advance: it can be one-third, one-half, or whatever the two of you agree is fair. Either way, reverse contingency fees give lawyers an incentive to produce the best possible result, Menendez says. Meanwhile, you get a lawyer to defend you without having to pay an hourly fee.

FYI: *Using a Lawyer . . . And What To Do If Things Go Wrong,* by Kay Ostberg (Random House, $8.95), includes a sample agreement and other no-nonsense tips. The book is available from HALT: Help Abolish Legal Tyranny at 202-887-8255. You can also find a client-friendly billing agreement on The Devil's Advocate Website (http://www.devilsadvocate.com).

Avoiding Legal Sticker Shock

FEAR OF RUNAWAY LEGAL FEES IS WHAT KEEPS MANY BUSINESS owners from getting the help they need or attracts them to low-cost options that wind up costing more in the long run. A better approach is to hire the best person for the task at hand, set a budget, and keep to it.

WHEN—IF EVER—DO YOU RECOMMEND SELF-HELP LEGAL MATERIALS?

Q 40 A GROWING NUMBER OF LEGAL SELF-HELP books and soft-ware packages enable small-business owners to understand the law and draft at least some legal documents themselves. These products are not a total substitute for competent legal help, but they can cut down on attorneys' fees for many common legal tasks, such as preparing incorporation papers, consulting agreements, and collection-demand letters. You'll find some of these materials referred to throughout this book.

Like practicing attorneys, self-help products vary widely in their attention to detail and their anticipation of business owners' needs. Choosing the right item depends on your specific legal concerns, the amount of instruction you require, and the time you're willing to devote to whatever do-it-yourself project you undertake. Many business owners would prefer focusing on running a company rather than being mired in self-help materials they only half understand.

Software packages come in two basic formats. Interactive programs take you through a series of on-screen questions, and then prepare a document that reflects your answers. While these programs are highly structured and sometimes inflexible, their hand-holding style generally makes them the easiest to use.

The other format is not truly software but consists simply of disks filled with files of legal-form templates that you can tailor with a word processor. To complete the forms, you delete the blank lines and add the pertinent information.

In an effort to be flexible while producing quality documents, self-help legal products run into a perennial conflict. While the interactive programs tend to limit your choices, they also prevent you from inserting or deleting clauses that might get you into legal trouble. Template-style packages that work with word processors offer greater flexibility but introduce additional risks of errors. For instance, while filling in the blanks you might add or delete words that could radically change the meaning of a document.

With all legal forms, it makes sense to read and understand the document before you sign and to consult a lawyer about any items in question. Since publishers have to produce documents that work in most states, they may not take account of all state-law differences; at best they tend to warn you when it might be wise to consult a lawyer.

In contrast, a local law firm can provide a tailored document for the jurisdiction where you do business. Sometimes (though you're not likely to know when), it has been "kitchen-tested" by others. The problem, of course, is that you pay dearly for that benefit, and often what you get is just a form generated by your lawyer's computer rather than your own.

Finally, sometimes the best-conceived legal self-help is no substitute for consulting an attorney. You're in over your head when you're unsure of legal strategies, if you can't understand the manual and on-line help no matter how many times you read it, or if you need to negotiate terms and don't know where to compromise.

80

TIP: Unfortunately, there's no credential or seal of approval to help you tell a good self-help product from a bad one. Look for materials geared to small businesses that come with instructions you can understand—either in print or on-line. Then, at least the first time you use the product, have your lawyer review whatever documents you prepare. Once a document (say a simple contract, independent contractor agreement, or a collection-demand letter) has your lawyer's blessing, you may be able to tailor it to other similar uses without having to consult an attorney each time.

IS THERE GOOD LEGAL ADVICE ON-LINE?

WHEN IT COMES TO USING THE INTERNET OR on-line services for legal matters, there's some good news and a lot of bad news right now. The good news: you can find many primary source materials (like court cases, state and federal laws, and regulations) for free through your home or office computer. The bad news: you can't rely on any of the advice you find that applies these materials. To be on the safe side, use on-line sources for background and to develop possible strategies—not as a lawyer substitute.

As with so much of what's on the Internet, on-line legal advice is only as good as the quality of what you retrieve. New developments in the law make frequent updates necessary. While responsible book publishers keep up with the changes by coming out with new editions, material can languish for years in cyberspace. It's sometimes hard to tell when what you download is hopelessly out of date. Nor does it necessarily account for rules that vary from state to state.

What's more, you probably know nothing about the motives or qualifications of those giving the tips. People use phony names and identities on-line. Lawyers rely on the Internet to solicit clients. It's difficult enough to evaluate the advice you get in person *(see Q46)*, let alone in this anonymous forum.

Even when you know a source means well and is highly credible, on-line communication is by nature quick and informal. Most often, you're not paying the lawyer who participates in an on-line bulletin board or chat room so, unlike a paying client, you can't expect quality service. I've noticed plenty of errors and outdated material in both on-line chats and other forms of posted advice—some of it from sources on whom I might rely in other contexts.

That said, on-line legal advice, like self-help legal books, can provide information about legal issues and help you identify potential problems that merit a lawyer's attention. If you decide to surf in legal waters, pay attention to who's offering the advice (if you can tell) and when it was posted. Here are some sites you might want to check out:

◆ **CourtTV Law Center (http://www.courttv.com).** The small-business area of this site includes articles on specific topics and a place to post questions (fielded by lawyers who tout their services). Before clicking on the links to other law-related sites, you can peruse the one-sentence abstract of what each one offers.

◆ **Legal Dot Net (http://www.legal.net).** The chief area of interest on this site is the "Dear Esquire" question-and-answer bulletin board. Here viewers can post queries and get quick responses from lawyers, at least some of whom hope to generate business. Much of the substance on this site deals with domestic relations or consumer law, but you're free to raise business law issues as well. These tend to be answered by a small handful of attorneys whose responses show up repeatedly. This site also provides links to a hodge-podge of other law-related sites, including those of organizations, law schools, and government agencies.

◆ **Law on the Net.** Operated by Nolo Press, the highly reputable publisher of many self-help law products, this site is accessible on America Online (keyword: Law Net) and on the World Wide Web (http://www.nolo.com). With links to other legal sites, it's a useful gateway to law on the Internet. You may also find it helpful to browse through the chat and message boards, which address questions that have concerned other business owners.

Most of the "experts" who participate are trying to sell you something, however. These include Nolo authors, whose shorthand answers to questions may generate interest in Nolo books. Lawyers surfing for clients also use this area to solicit business on-line.

◆ **'Lectric Law Library (http://www.lectlaw.com).** This sprawling site, which combines law and whimsy, includes several areas of interest to small businesses. Both "The Business Law Lounge" and "The Reference Room" have articles on a wide range of topics. Some give the name of the author and the date the article was posted; others are attributed only to 'Lectric Law Library. Another area, called "The Forms Room," contains dozens of business legal forms, unfortunately without any information about adapting them to your own use.

SHOULD I USE A PREPAID LEGAL SERVICES PLAN?

 IF YOU ALREADY HAVE SPECIFIC LEGAL NEEDS (like drafting a contract or handling a collection matter), your time would probably be better spent shopping for a good lawyer.

Prepaid legal services plans designed specifically for small businesses provide access to a lawyer for a yearly fee of roughly $150 to $350. Matters covered range from simple contracts to equipment leases to accounts-receivable collection work, and there is generally no restriction on the frequency with which subscribers can use the service. These plans are not likely to take the place of your regular lawyer. Still, on many matters you can get a quick answer without having to worry about a separate bill.

Though coverage and fees differ from plan to plan, most include drafting of simple legal documents (a bill of sale or a power of attorney, for example) and follow-up letters or phone calls to third parties. A particularly valuable benefit is unlimited telephone consultation, which is enough to resolve many small-business matters. Still, the quality of advice you get is only as good as the person answering the phone. Chances are that individual doesn't know your business.

Prepaid plans are not appropriate for all legal matters. They rarely cover admiralty or securities cases, for example, or elaborate, customized contracts like marketing or technical agreements. Lawsuits generally cost extra and may be handled through referrals to local lawyers at an additional charge.

If you decide to cover some of your legal needs this way, it's best to go through trade and professional groups and local chambers of commerce. Many offer plans uniquely tailored to the business needs of their members at reduced group rates. The other option is dealing with a private nationwide vendor. But for a variety of reasons, these companies haven't been very successful in serving—or marketing to—the small-business market.

Depending on the policy, prepaid legal service plans designed for individuals or families—much more common than those designed for businesses—may cover some of your company needs. A better choice, though, is a firm experienced in small-business matters. Here are some other questions to ask before selecting a plan:

◆ Are the attorneys skilled in a variety of different practice areas?

◆ How many years of experience do they have? (Five years or more is best.)

◆ Do the lawyers cover the locale in which your company operates?

◆ Which services are covered by the plan and which ones cost extra?

◆ How can you contact the service (generally they have 800-number telephone hotlines).

◆ Does the plan permit you to change lawyers or drop the service if you're not satisfied?

TIP: Since there's no oversight group specifically assigned to monitor the quality of these plans, it's important to select one with its own procedure for handling complaints. Before you sign on, check the firm's reputation in your area by calling the Better Business Bureau, Consumer Affairs Office, and state Attorney General's office. The National Resource Center for Consumers of Legal Services, a nonprofit research and education group in Gloucester, Virginia, at 804-693-9330 (http://www.nrccls.org), operates as a clearing house for information about these plans. Choose one that has operated locally for at least two years without complaints.

ARE THERE ANY CUT-RATE DEALS FOR LAWYERS?

 ALTHOUGH THESE SERVICES ARE RARE, THEY DO exist. Local bar associations, especially in large cities, often operate lawyer referral services, including free ("pro bono") help for certain matters. The District of Columbia Bar Association in Washington, D.C. (202-737-4700; Website: http://www.dcbar.org), operates several such "community outreach" programs. One, run by the Computer and Technology Law Section, offers two hours of free counseling to small and minority high-tech companies. Volunteer lawyers field questions about intellectual property, employment law, contracts, and business structures.

Another similar service is Volunteer Lawyers for the Arts in New York City, which caters to low-income artists (including writers, actors, and filmmakers). Matters covered include copyright, contract review, and estate planning. VLA fields quick questions through a free telephone hotline at 212-319-2910. For more complex issues, it refers callers to pro bono attorneys; VLA charges a nominal administrative fee (typically $30 to $50 per matter), but clients pay nothing for the attorney's time.

Far more common are discounted rates on legal fees available to members of some trade associations. Often they take the form of referrals coupled with "advice and discount" deals: you get a free initial consultation by phone or in person (typically half an hour to an hour), plus discounts on that lawyer's future services. It's not a bad way to see the lawyer in action before committing to a more longer-term relationship.

HOW CAN I REDUCE THE NUMBER OF SURPRISES ON THE NEXT LEGAL BILL?

Q 44 MOST LEGAL BILLS HAVE TWO SECTIONS: CHARGES for the lawyer's time and an itemized list of expenses. Here are 10 ways to reduce the number of billable hours you ring up and keep other costs to a minimum:

1 **Dispense with the pleasantries.** When you're paying by the hour, the meter's running on every conversation. So it's best to skip small talk and get right to substance. This is easier by phone than in person. If you must meet (*see 5, below*), schedule appointments for specific time periods (say, 30 minutes or an hour), and clock the meeting so you don't go over that limit.

2 **Educate yourself.** Use this book and materials referred to throughout it for background. You'll get a basic understanding of the issues and know what questions to ask. This cuts down on the time and money you'll spend having the lawyer explain basic legal principles.

3 **Make your goals clear.** At the end of each conversation, discuss the next step. Don't assume the lawyer knows best or adopt an attitude of "anything you say," or you may get stuck paying for services you don't want or need. To avoid misunderstandings, send a follow-up note outlining your concerns.

4 **Keep the lawyer behind the scenes.** Having the lawyer coach you behind the scenes rather than appearing on the front line is sometimes a great way to cut costs and keep business dealings low-key. Unless you're totally tongue-tied, you can negotiate basic agreements, send correspondence,

and even resolve conflicts directly with other business executives. You'll probably want to involve the lawyer more visibly when the other side brings in their attorney; the legal principles are complex; or it would strengthen your bargaining power to have someone do the talking for you.

5 Avoid meetings. Your goal here is to reduce the time your lawyer spends meeting with you and with others on your behalf. Unless you're going over complex documents or would gain a strategic advantage face-to-face, most business can take place by phone, fax, or letter. Busy lawyers will respect this approach.

6 Organize relevant documents. Write a memo (including an index) summarizing the contents of documents you turn over to your lawyer. This cuts down on the time he or she must spend wading through masses of paper.

7 Brief your lawyer in writing. Before phoning or visiting with anything more than a quick question, send your lawyer a short memo (ideally one page or less). Summarize the key facts, the business concerns at stake (for instance, your desire not to jeopardize key relationships), and any legal questions you've spotted.

8 Help your lawyer be efficient. Unless you're up against a deadline or a deal is moving quickly, don't call for daily progress reports. If a question isn't urgent, wait until you have a few items to discuss and cover them all at once. Before placing a call, make notes to yourself about what you plan to ask.

TIP: Rick Riebesell, a Denver lawyer who does a lot of work with entrepreneurs, suggests you avoid what he calls "professional-to-professional" time—asking your lawyer to talk to your accountant, for instance. At that point, "you have two meters running instead of one," he notes. "No one knows if the two professionals charge you for 20 minutes while they talk about their golf game."

9 Let the lawyer know you're pinching pennies. Just sensitizing the lawyer to your cost concerns may help deter unnecessary spending and keep those billable hours lean.

Also alert the lawyer to what a business deal (or potential legal battle) is worth to you. You don't want the lawyer's bill to be so high that it's not cost effective for you to close the deal or assert your rights.

Don't be afraid that you'll look cheap by proposing specific cost-control measures. Ask that midlevel associates (lawyers with three to five years' experience) be assigned to do any research that's necessary and that your attorney rely on para-legals *(see Q35)* for routine paperwork; in most cases their time costs a lot less than you'd pay for a more senior-level lawyer working on the matter.

Another money saver: keep photocopies and faxes to a minimum. Law firms routinely mark up this service. When there's a lot of copying to be done, offer to have one of your own staff do it.

If travel is essential, make clear that you expect all costs to be itemized, including a breakdown of the incidentals on hotel bills (like laundry, health club, and room service charges). Ask your lawyer to use the least costly mode of ground transportation, whether that's a taxi or a rental car. Offer to buy your lawyer's airline tickets (giving you or your travel agent a chance to shop for the best deals), rather than reimbursing the firm after the money has been spent.

TIP: An occasional bill for a cellular phone call is acceptable, but if your lawyer can only find time to handle your case on the fly, you might question whether you're getting the service you're paying for.

TIP: Make clear that you want to be billed for expenses at cost, rather than at a markup, John Toothman advises. Out-going faxes should be free; the charge for incoming ones shouldn't exceed the cost of the paper (no more than 25 cents a page). For photocopies, 10 or 15 cents a page is reasonable, Toothman says.

TIP: Within reason, work-related meals are legitimate. But watch out for frequent meal charges and cab rides home when a lawyer works late. Especially at large firms in big cities, junior-level lawyers sometimes abuse the privilege and bill their dinners to unsuspecting clients.

10 Don't pay a premium for expedited services. Unless it's really a rush, don't let your lawyer get carried away with faxes, couriers, and overnight mail, all of which usually cost extra. By having overnight mail billed to your own account, rather than to the law firm's, you avoid the inevitable markup or potentially higher rates the firm charges. (Many overnight carriers offer discounts for small businesses.)

Better yet, when time is of the essence and confidentiality isn't an issue, log onto e-mail. Many lawyers now use it, but their firms haven't quite figured out how to charge for it. The same document that costs $20 to receive by fax or overnight mail might be sent to you by e-mail for free.

TIP: It's best to specify that you not be billed for overtime for secretaries and paralegals, since these charges are subject to abuse. Some support staff find excuses to work late because they want the money. Likewise, law firms sometimes use "overtime" as an excuse for overbilling clients.

ANY TIPS FOR CUTTING LITIGATION EXPENSES?

Q 45 EMPHASIZE YOUR DESIRE FOR EARLY SETTLE-ment, which usually saves money. Require the lawyer to submit a budget (subject to your approval) for expenses, covering such things as travel and hiring expert witnesses (like doctors, appraisers, and engineers). Make clear that you want to be billed for these and other items at cost, rather than at a markup.

When you need expert witnesses, offer to hire them directly, rather than going through a service, which typically tacks on a finder's fee. You can also help locate witnesses yourself, cutting down on the law firm services you'll be charged for. One method is to call lawyers who've handled similar cases and ask them for recommendations. Alternatively, you can use industry contacts to come up with experts of your own.

Instead of paying graphic artists to prepare courtroom exhibits, consider a more "homegrown" approach. Many software presentation programs enable even neophytes to prepare professional-looking charts and graphs. Getting permission to reprint (in enlarged form) illustrations from books may be another option.

There are also a number of ways to avoid excessive court reporters' fees associated with depositions (sworn testimony before trial). Suggest your lawyer take only the essential ones, rather than using the shotgun approach that some attorneys favor. To reduce travel costs, consider videotaping out-of-town depositions. Then decide which depositions you absolutely must have transcribed. For those you need, offer to share costs with other lawyers in the case or to buy copies of transcripts they've ordered.

Managing Your Lawyer

CHANCES ARE YOU'RE MUCH TOO BUSY TO BE SECOND-guessing your lawyer at every turn. But you don't want to take a backseat to what's happening either.

HOW CAN I EVALUATE THE QUALITY OF SERVICE I'M GETTING?

BE AN ACTIVE PARTICIPANT IN YOUR LEGAL matter. Hang on to the originals of any documents you submit to your lawyer and get duplicates of any documents your lawyer sends out on your behalf. This will keep you informed about the case. If you wind up switching lawyers at some point, your files will be complete.

Meanwhile, keep abreast of everything that's going on, including deadlines. Accompany your lawyer to critical meetings and court appearances. His or her behavior around other members of the profession—and reactions to it—may supply valuable clues about whether or not your lawyer has the respect of peers.

Also ask to see copies of any correspondence or court papers before they're sent out, so you can raise questions and make suggestions. Be sure you agree with what they say. Don't hesitate to press for information until you fully understand the legal strategy and are satisfied with the tack.

At key junctures, or if you think your case isn't being handled properly, you might want to get a second opinion. This would be appropriate, for example, if you're trying to decide whether to accept a substantial settlement offer. Lawyers gambling on a huge verdict (and the publicity that goes with it) might be tempted to turn the offer down. Given the risks—and the lawyer's vested interest—it's a good idea to seek a consultation with a disinterested party. Most lawyers will gladly cooperate.

WHAT CAN I DO IF I'M FED UP WITH MY LAWYER?

Q 47 MOST DISPUTES BETWEEN LAWYERS AND CLIENTS fall into one (or more) of the following categories: disappointment with the result; dissatisfaction with the service; and outrage about the fees. Many of these problems can be avoided with the preventive measures outlined in this chapter. When these fail, it's best to resolve conflicts early on, rather than allowing problems to fester. Here are some of the common complaints about lawyers and what you can do about them:

◆ **Angry about the result.** With the recent litigation explosion, more people are becoming disillusioned with lawyers. Some wind up in court against the very lawyers who handled their cases.

There are many reasons why that can happen. Occasionally, the case starts with an unscrupulous lawyer who promises the moon or a client who can't accept the disappointment of losing. Far more often, the attorney isn't knowledgeable enough about an area of law and makes a major mistake, misses a deadline, or doesn't pursue all the obvious allegations.

If you think your lawyer has messed up, it's a good idea to get a second opinion. It may be that the most economical course of action is to cut your losses—to settle the case, for instance, rather than pursuing it through trial and appeal.

Though most lawyers will gladly give a consultation at this late stage, it's a rare breed of lawyer who'll represent you in a suit against a fellow attorney. These cases are also hard to win: you have to prove not only that the lawyer was remiss, but that the attorney's negligence caused you financial loss. Even if you get a judgment against your former lawyer, you may have trouble collecting it if he or she doesn't have malpractice insurance. The battle might not make financial sense.

FYI: Should you decide to go the malpractice route, the book *If You Want to Sue a Lawyer,* by Kay Ostberg, includes a directory of lawyers specializing in such cases. It's available for $10 from HALT, an Organization of Americans for Legal Reform, at 202-887-8255.

◆ **Not getting enough attention.** Chances are your lawyer, just like the rest of us, is juggling many matters at a time. Yet few things are more infuriating when you're waiting to close a deal or get a conflict resolved than to have your lawyer suddenly tied up with other people's "emergencies." Maybe the lawyer hasn't returned phone calls promptly, didn't take the usual care in drafting documents, or hasn't kept you up to date about the status of your case.

The best time to raise these and other concerns is when they first start to irk you. You have a right to have your calls returned the same day or, in extreme cases (your lawyer is in court or on the road), the next day. You're also entitled to the best-quality work product.

For every time-consuming task that you turn over to your lawyer, check that he or she is able to handle it. If not, offer to take this piece of business elsewhere. Then set reasonable deadlines about when you expect each phase to be completed.

If that day arrives and the work isn't done, call for a status report. Ask the lawyer what's been done so far, what remains to be done, what you can do to expedite things, and how much more time the matter will take.

When you can't get satisfaction, you always have the option of switching lawyers, but it's best not to do that in the middle of a deal or a lawsuit. Among other things, the lawyer could stick you with a hefty bill for work so far and leave you with little to show for it.

Should you decide to make the switch while a matter is pending, be sure to do it in writing. Be specific about the date on which you received the last services, so you won't be charged for work done after that.

◆ **Being overcharged.** This may be the most common complaint and the most preventable *(see Q44)*. Your best defense is to have a written fee agreement *(see Q39)* and to carefully check all bills.

Before you ever receive that dreaded invoice, you should have a rough idea of the time your lawyer has spent on your matter. Jot down the dates of any phone calls or meetings and how long they took. Save copies of all correspondence or documents the lawyer drafted.

When you get the bill, compare it with your own tally, just as you'd audit a credit card bill. Ask the lawyer to explain any expenses that seem unusual (you shouldn't be charged for routine secretarial work, local phone calls, or office supplies, for instance). If the fee for a particular service exceeds what you've paid in the not-too-distant past, question it. For matters that have spanned more than one billing period, add the current charges to what you've paid so far and see whether the total seems reasonable.

Most lawyers abhor fee disputes and will make every effort to resolve them promptly. If that fails, you may have to resort to more formal dispute resolution methods—preferably with fee agreement in hand. The options include arbitration *(see Q97)*, if your fee agreement provides for it, state rules require it, or the lawyer will submit to it voluntarily. Better yet, the lawyer may agree to mediation *(see Q97)*. The last resort is a lawsuit.

TIP: "A proper bill should tell you who does what, when, and why," John Toothman says. If the only entry is "for services rendered," you'll want specifics. To avoid surprises, you can ask to see a sample statement before you hire the lawyer.

TIP: Don't be afraid that asking about questionable charges will sour the relationship or make you seem cheap. My lawyer sends a cover letter with each invoice suggesting I call him with any questions about it. On the one occasion when I did, there turned out to be a clerical error: two extra zeros had been added to the charge for faxes.

WHAT RECOURSE DO I HAVE IF MY LAWYER HAS BEEN UNETHICAL?

Q 48 MOST STATES HAVE ADOPTED A UNIFORM SET OF standards governing lawyers' conduct. The ultimate sanction is getting a lawyer disciplined or disbarred (having his or her license revoked). To do that, you would report the lawyer to the state agency that licenses attorneys or oversees their conduct. The name of the agency varies from state to state. It might be called something like the grievance committee, disciplinary committee, or office of attorney ethics. Call the state bar association to locate the right place to file your complaint.

As a practical matter, though, lawyers have been notoriously lax—and secretive—about policing their own. Unless your lawyer has committed a crime, consistently been incompetent, or abused drugs or alcohol, you probably have little recourse.

One of the major problems that comes up involves conflicts of interest. These are situations in which work from one client (including access to confidential information) interferes with a lawyer's ability to be fair or honest in representing another.

When potential conflicts arise, the lawyer has an ethical obligation to tell you and to give you the option of finding another attorney. Should you discover conflicts the lawyer hasn't mentioned, there may be little you can do besides taking your business elsewhere. When the lawyer has committed fraud you might be able to sue, but to make it worth your while, you should have suffered substantial damages.

Most other grievances that you submit to a state agency will probably go into a file; generally, only if a number of other people make the same complaint will the authorities take action. Even if you have the satisfaction of seeing the attorney reprimanded (or disbarred), you probably won't collect a cent.

There is one exception: some states have established client security trust funds to help compensate people whose lawyers have stolen money from them. If you've had this misfortune, you may be able to recover at least part of what you've lost.

FYI: *Taming The Lawyers,* by Kenneth Menendez (Merritt Publishing, $19.95), is a practical guide to preventing problems with your lawyer when you bring a lawsuit.

Mad at Your Lawyer, by Tanya Starnes, a malpractice lawyer in Emeryville, California (Nolo Press, $21.95), is a consumer-oriented handbook covering everything that could possibly go wrong and what to do about it.

CHAPTER 4

Hiring and Managing Employees

ORKING WITH PEOPLE WHO often feel like family is one of the attractions of being a small-business owner. But unfortunately you're still vulnerable to lawsuits by current and former employees. These cases have become increasingly common, and they're some of the most costly legal claims now plaguing businesses large and small.

Several factors contribute to the trend. One is the growing number of federal, state, and local laws covering the worker-boss relationship. Another is the declining sense of company loyalty stemming from widespread layoffs and downsizing. Worse yet are the reports of giant jury verdicts that periodically make headlines. While these awards are rare and usually get reversed on appeal, most workers never hear that part of the story. Instead, they think suing the boss is even better than winning the lottery. It can cost companies a lot of money to dispel the myth.

Big companies can drag out a case for years, because they can afford to pay expensive lawyers to defend them. Small companies don't have that luxury. Losing an employment case could take a huge financial toll: in 1996 the median award in cases for wrongful termination and constructive discharge (when a worker is forced out) was $205,794 according to Jury Verdict Research, of Horsham, Pennsylvania. Even if the company ultimately prevails, just defending the suit could cost tens or even hundreds of thousands of dollars in legal fees. The same goes for the hefty settlements that a company can get strong-armed into paying.

The good news is that most workplace disputes are avoidable with good management and minimal help from a lawyer.

Don't assume that you're so small that key laws don't cover your operations. True, some federal statutes apply only to businesses of a certain size: the Civil Rights Act, and the Americans with Disabilities Act (companies with 15 or more employees); the Age Discrimination in Employment Act, and the Consolidated Omnibus Budget Reconciliation Act, or COBRA (20 or more workers); and the Family and Medical Leave Act (50 or more employees). But many states have their own laws that address some of the same issues, and they may well apply to smaller shops. Even if they don't, it's important to know right from wrong as you grow and plan for the future.

Likewise, some preventive measures might seem more appropriate for much larger companies—adopting a written sexual harassment policy, for instance, telling your staff in writing about the rules for using computer equipment, or distributing an employee handbook. Yet here too, it pays to run your business like a much larger operation. Legally sound personnel practices don't have to compromise the intimate workplace that you cherish. In fact, they can prevent the kinds of disputes that threaten to tear it apart.

Hiring Smart

TAKE A LOOK AT THE WAY YOU SEEK OUT QUALIFIED candidates. Your hiring practices might draw legal fire from the applicants you turn down. Someone who gets the job and later sues for discrimination in employment might also complain about illegal things you did at the hiring stage.

WHAT CAN'T I SAY IN HELP-WANTED ADS?

SPECIFYING MORE EDUCATION THAN YOU NEED (with terms like "Ivy type" or "college grad") tends to exclude people who might be able to do the work without meeting these particular requirements. Calls for individuals with limited experience (for instance, "recent grad") could imply that you're discriminating against older workers.

In general, avoid wording that implies a prejudice against a so-called "protected class" covered by antidiscrimination laws (sex, race, religion, nationality, age, or disability) advises

Helene M. Freeman, a lawyer with Dorsey & Whitney in New York City. By stating that your company is "an equal opportunity employer" you "are indicating that members of a protected class are welcome to apply," Freeman says. That alone won't protect you from legal claims, she adds, but it may help.

Since many older workers are being laid off or taking early retirement, watch out for potential age discrimination lawsuits by people over 40. Capable individuals who notice ads for people who are "energetic" might read age bias between the lines.

Sex-based job titles like "gal Friday," "salesman," or "waitress" express gender preferences. When drafting ads, you're less likely to spark a complaint or legal action with sex-neutral terms like "clerical assistant," "sales representative," "warehouse person," or "individual to wait on tables."

The best defense against legal challenge is an ad that explicitly describes the job skills needed and includes a brief listing of responsibilities. To attract an experienced person, advertise for the proficiency you need: "careful proofreader," "capable writer," or "good communicator."

Avoid including numbers among the qualifications, whether they be the number of years' experience or the age of the applicant. Instead, focus on the precise abilities you need. An ad for a "talented marketing manager" is more likely to draw the person you are looking for than an ad that simply calls for someone of a certain age or with "three to five years of experience," for instance. Don't demand an advanced degree unless a specific aspect of a college education is needed to do the job.

Before placing any ad—including one written by an agency or recruiter—have an employment lawyer screen the text to determine whether it could be misinterpreted.

Finally, says Freeman, be sure your hiring procedures are consistent with what you've expressed on paper. If a man responds to your ad for a clerical assistant, don't steer him to an opening for a stockroom job, for example; and a woman who wants to be a bartender won't welcome a suggestion that she wait on tables.

TIP: If space permits, a brief listing of responsibilities in your help-wanted ad can intrigue potential applicants and attract capable individuals.

TIP: Phrases like "supplement your pension" could be read as a call for retired workers, even if all you mean to say is that the job is part-time. If this is true, say so, by indicating that the job can be done part-time, on a freelance basis, 20 hours per week, or as weekend work.

WHAT QUESTIONS IS IT ILLEGAL FOR ME TO ASK JOB APPLICANTS?

Q 50 "HOW OLD ARE YOU?" "WHAT COUNTRY ARE YOU from?" "Do you have children?" These might be suitable topics for social gatherings, but they are off-limits when you're hiring employees. Various state and federal laws make it illegal to ask such questions or to inquire about race, sex, or disabilities. Other no-no's: "Do you plan to have children?" "Are you married?" "Do you go to church?" Even indirect questions, perhaps about family or someone's personal life, could be a "legal minefield," says Bettina B. Plevan, a lawyer with Proskauer Rose in New York City. Some local ordinances, such as those in New York City and San Francisco, ban queries about sexual orientation. Businesses that raise taboo topics risk costly discrimination lawsuits from job applicants who charge that they were denied positions because of their responses.

When interviewing, focus on whether a person can do the work, Plevan advises. Let's say the job includes a hectic travel schedule. You might wonder whether someone of a certain age can keep up the pace or if a woman in her childbearing years can be away overnight. Don't ask, "At this stage in your life can you travel a lot?" or "Do you have a baby-sitter or a spouse who shares child-care responsibilities?" Instead, say: "This job involves overnight travel at least once a week. Are you going to have any difficulty with that?"

The same approach applies to illnesses or disabilities. If a job applicant uses a wheelchair, it's illegal to ask, "How did you become disabled?" or "Do you have a disability that would interfere with your ability to perform the job?" Legal phrasing would be: "Can you perform the functions of this job with reasonable accommodation?" or "Can you meet the attendance requirements of this job?" or "Do you have the required licenses to do the work?"

Federal regulations say that employers "may not ask about the existence, nature, or severity of a disability" before making someone a job offer. As a rule, don't ask questions you wouldn't ask of all candidates, says Plevan. Even if job applicants volunteer information about their disabilities, you may not follow up with requests for more detail.

To steer clear of problems, update your company's job-application form by eliminating illegal questions, such as those about date of birth and marital status, injuries, and illnesses. Teach people involved in hiring how to avoid prohibited subjects. Of course, you want to be friendly toward the person you are interviewing and to evaluate whether you would enjoy working together. Questions about experience, previous positions, and education—provided a certain level of schooling is needed to do the job—are all fair game. That leaves you and a job applicant lots to talk about without treading on what's illegal.

WHAT ARE MY OBLIGATIONS UNDER THE AMERICANS WITH DISABILITIES ACT?

Q 51 THIS LAW, WHICH APPLIES TO COMPANIES WITH 15 or more employees, covers all aspects of the work relationship, from hiring to firing. People protected include those with a physical or mental impairment that "substantially limits a major life activity" such as hearing, seeing, speaking, walking, or performing manual tasks.

The ADA does not require you to hire people who can't do the job. The law states that a person must be able to perform the "essential functions" of the position with "reasonable accommodation." In applying this rule, the Equal Employment Opportunity Commission (EEOC), the agency responsible for enforcing the employment-related sections of ADA, considers the manner in which past employees in the same job performed particular tasks and the time it took them.

At the job interview, it's illegal to ask applicants whether they have disabilities (*see Q50*) or require candidates with disabilities to take a medical exam before you make a job offer. If an offer is contingent on a physical, that must be your policy for all candidates, not just the person with the disability.

Once you hire someone with a disability (or if one of your current staff develops one) it's illegal to fire the person or reduce health insurance for people with disabilities. You also will have to make the reasonable accommodation that the law requires. What's "reasonable" varies from company to company, and both management and employees must be willing to negotiate the necessary accommodations.

The law says that accommodating workers with disabilities need not cause the company an "undue hardship." While there are no set rules about what that means, the EEOC will consider the company's size and financial condition in deciding whether discrimination has taken place. To help avoid problems, it's a good idea to identify the essential functions of a job in a written description before you hire.

Another ounce of prevention involves employees returning to work after an illness or injury. Here it's important to avoid the parting remark, "Call me when you're fully recovered." The ADA requires you to make reasonable accommodations for individuals with disabilities who want to return to work before they are completely able to do their regular jobs.

One way to satisfy the law is by eliminating marginal responsibilities that the person is unable to handle (with a cashier, for instance, that might be restocking shelves). Another possibility is taking steps to help someone do the essential functions of the job—perhaps rearranging furniture to make the employee's immediate work space wheelchair-accessible. You need not create new jobs, but the law may require you to reassign workers (even if it means a pay cut). For example, a person who is recovering from a repetitive stress injury and cannot type may be assigned other administrative duties. Call the federal Disability and Business Technical Assistance Center for free telephone advice at 800-949-4232.

TIP: Making reasonable accommodations doesn't have to break the bank or put a company out of business, says Rick Douglas, executive director of the President's Committee on Employment of People with Disabilities, which offers free telephone advice through its Job Accommodation Network at 800-ADA-WORK. Most modifications cost less than $500, and some are surprisingly low-tech. For instance, removing the top drawer can make a desk accessible to someone who uses a wheelchair. Employers of people with chronic conditions might develop work schedules that include rest periods. For more ideas, consult the Job Accommodation Network or the EEOC's free Technical Assistance Manual (to order a copy, call 800-669-3362).

FYI: Many government-enforcement actions brought under the Americans with Disabilities Act have involved one or more of the following blunders:
◆ Asking a job applicant about his or her impairment
◆ Requiring a candidate with a disability to have a medical exam
◆ Reducing health insurance for an employee with a particular infirmity
◆ Firing a staff member who develops a disability.

WHEN ARE DRUG TESTS LEGAL?

 DRUG TESTING IS A CONTROVERSIAL AND evolving field, with associated morale and legal problems. For workers in certain industries (like airline pilots and other transportation employees whose jobs affect public safety), federal law requires you test. More often, business owners are left to set—and administer—their own policies. That makes them vulnerable to lawsuits for invasion of privacy *(see Q65)*.

Given the risks, most lawyers discourage random testing of current employees for drugs (or alcohol). As a rule, it's prudent to limit random testing to workers whose positions involve public safety, says Robert Naeve, a lawyer with Morrison & Foerster in Irvine, California. For example, if your employees drive commercial trucks and other vehicles, federal regulations may require random drug tests. Workers who carry guns might also have to submit to random testing under certain circumstances. And if your business involves government contracts, they sometimes call for random testing of your staff.

However, you can generally order an employee to submit to a drug test if you have "reasonable suspicion" that he or she is abusing unlawful drugs or controlled substances, says Naeve. Should the test be positive, the test and any resulting discipline are likely to be upheld if the employee sues for invasion of privacy, he says.

The trouble is, lawyers disagree about what constitutes reasonable suspicion. Naeve, who recommends managers be trained to recognize signs of substance abuse, would strictly limit testing to cases in which employees look to be abusing (for example, they have a staggered gait, dilated pupils, or smell of marijuana). Outside of California, a state with strict privacy protections, some lawyers say drug testing might be prompted by behavior such as falling asleep on the job, shortness of attention, or an increase in workplace accidents.

If drug testing seems the way to go, adopt a written policy and get employees to acknowledge it in writing. This sets the rules and puts your staff on notice about what to expect. That alone will not protect you in the event of a lawsuit, but it could help your defense. Rules vary enormously from state to state, however, so it's best to have an employment lawyer prepare and implement a drug policy.

For job applicants, most courts have ruled that across-the-board testing is okay, Naeve says, but here, too, it's best to exercise a few precautions. Extend a conditional offer of employment before you ask people to take the test, do the test prior to the first day of work (so you'll have the results before someone is on board), and be sure you require the test of all applicants in the same job category.

TIP: Find out whether your state has a law on confidentiality of medical information. If so, determine whether it applies to drug testing in the employment context and what steps are required for you to comply.

TIP: When conducting any drug test, be sure to use the least intrusive means possible: it's good employee relations, lessens the likelihood of a lawsuit, and can help your case if you're sued. So if you're worried that an employee will alter samples submitted for a urine test, require workers to remove their jackets and empty their pockets instead of having an observer or video record every move. Asking what prescription medicine an employee has been taking is usually permissible (and sometimes necessary to evaluate test results), but asking why the employee has been taking those drugs can sometimes lead to problems. Don't risk a defamation lawsuit by communicating the test results—which could be false-positive—to people who don't need to know.

SHOULD MY COMPANY HAVE AN ANTINEPOTISM POLICY?

 ANTINEPOTISM POLICIES ARE LEGAL IN MOST states, says Robert Heiferman, a lawyer with Jackson, Lewis, Schnitzler & Krupman in White Plains, New York. Yet there's a growing trend, especially in California, for courts to rule that these policies discriminate on the basis of marital or family status and also violate employees' privacy rights.

In states where such policies are allowed, Heiferman discourages business owners from adopting strict antinepotism rules. The reason: good workers are hard to find, and staffers can be a source of referrals. If you employ family members in those jurisdictions, however, you should avoid hiring managers' relatives and should not allow employees to supervise their kin. Such situations can lead to morale problems and allegations of favoritism, he says.

TIP: Heiferman suggests using the following language, which you can include in your employee handbook *(see Q60)*, or distribute separately: "In order to maintain impartiality and fairness in employee relations, [company name] does not hire relatives of employees when it would result in one family member working under the direct or indirect supervision or authority of another family member."

Defining Relationships

WHEN MOST BUSINESS OWNERS THINK ABOUT STAFFING their operations, they focus on economics—whether it makes the most financial sense to hire employees or to rely on consultants, for instance. But how you fill those personnel needs also can have significant legal consequences for both workers and business owners.

WHAT'S THE DIFFERENCE BETWEEN AN EMPLOYEE AND AN INDEPENDENT CONTRACTOR?

 LAWYERS AND STATE AND FEDERAL AGENCIES CONtinue to wrestle with this question. On some level, most tests look at how much control (both physical and financial) you have over the person doing the work.

The clearest examples of consultants (sometimes called freelancers, contractors, or temps) are people who work for a number of different clients, operate out of their own offices, and set their own hours. Some of the items that tilt the scale toward "employee" are: working for one employer at a time, working on the company's premises, receiving regular payments at fixed intervals, and being required to follow the company's instructions about work.

Whether someone is an employee or a freelancer can make a big difference in your bottom line. With freelancers, you don't usually have to pay overtime; Social Security, unemployment, and Medicare taxes; and workers' compensation, unemployment, or disability insurance premiums. These are costs you generally must shell out for employees.

FYI: By February 28 of each year you must file tax form 1099-MISC with the IRS, reporting income paid to every independent contractor during the previous year *(see Q121)*. Freelancers must receive their copy of the form by January 31. You're required to file this form for any independent contractor who's not a corporation if you paid this person or company $600 or more during the prior year.

For every person who's classified as a temp, rather than a staffer, the IRS loses Social Security taxes. So not surprisingly, the agency is cracking down on companies that try to duck tax obligations by labeling as "freelancers" people who work side by side with full-time employees.

When going after companies for back taxes (plus penalties), the IRS applies a number of criteria to figure out whether a business is labeling employees as independent contractors *(see table on pages 110-11)*. Unfortunately, none of these factors by itself is conclusive. Instead, the agency looks at each case separately to determine the type of relationship.

Another important issue to consider: fewer legal obligations automatically surround your relationship with independent contractors. Unlike employees, they're not entitled to overtime, time off for family or medical emergencies, or protections against discrimination based on race, sex, nationality, religion, age, or disability.

By dealing with independent contractors, therefore, you're less prone to employment lawsuits—say for wrongful termination or discrimination. The flip side is that you're bound by whatever agreement you make with independent contractors. Break that contract, and you might have to pay damages. In contrast, employees don't usually have contracts with their bosses, leaving you generally free to fire them for any reason that doesn't violate the law *(see Q57)*.

TIP: One area where you may be more vulnerable to lawsuits involves on-the-job injuries. When employees are covered by workers' compensation, they can't sue you for such injuries but can only collect benefits from workers' comp. With freelancers, your liability is much broader, so you'll want to be sure your insurance covers it *(see Q16)*.

WHEN SHOULD I HIRE EMPLOYEES INSTEAD OF FREELANCERS?

THIS IS A BUSINESS DECISION AS WELL AS A legal one. Here are some things to consider:

◆ **Staffing requirements.** With independent contractors, you can hire just the help you need, when you need

Employee or Independent Contractor?

SOME FACTORS THE IRS CONSIDERS

EMPLOYEES

Must follow the boss's instructions about when, where, and how to work.

May be trained to do the work a certain way.

Likely to be reimbursed for business expenses.

Generally paid at regular intervals—by the hour, week, or month.

Get paid whether or not the company makes money.

Might have a benefits package covering items like vacation pay, sick pay, life insurance.

Have a continuing relationship with the company.

Are free to quit at any time without further obligations.

Work for one employer at a time.

Provide services that are a key part of the employer's regular business.

it. That assumes you can do without having someone at your disposal on a continuing basis, though. If not, you might rather have the work done in-house.

◆ **Cost.** Since they must pay their own overhead, independent contractors typically charge 30 to 50 percent more than what you'd pay an employee to do the same work. Still, you can reap huge savings by being able to retain people only when you need them. Nor do you have many of the expenses associated with employees, including benefits, overhead, overtime, Social Security and Medicare taxes, workers' compensation, and state unemployment or disability insurance premiums. When consultants' fees exceed what you'd pay a

Control most—if not all—aspects of how the work gets done.

Rely on their own methods for doing the work.

Usually incur fixed costs (like office rent and telephone) regardless of work being performed.

Tend to be paid by the project (lawyers are a major exception).

Can make a profit or a loss.

Buy their own insurance. Don't get paid for time not worked.

Are retained for specific projects or periods.

Depending on the deal, may have an obligation to finish the job.

Have more than one client.

Are not integrally involved in company's day-to-day operations.

111

full-time (or part-time) staff member, you might think about hiring someone instead.

◆ **Intellectual property.** When someone is your employee, you automatically own the rights to anything he or she creates "in the scope of employment" *(see Q21)*. With independent contractors, the scale usually tips the other way *(see Q21)*. You can address this subject in a written agreement *(see Q56)* that requires the consultant to transfer some (if not all) rights in his or her work. But depending on how much bargaining power you both have, you may not be able to get all the rights you'd like.

TIP: Since they work for a variety of clients, independent contractors have competing loyalties. And particularly with people you don't know well, there's a risk of trade secrets leaking out. You can reduce this risk by checking references and having consultants sign confidentiality agreements *(see Q31).*

SHOULD I ASK INDEPENDENT CONTRACTORS TO SIGN A WRITTEN AGREEMENT?

YES. HAVING A WRITTEN AGREEMENT CAN HELP clarify your relationship and provide you with a lot of legal protection. It's one factor state and federal agencies will consider when there's any dispute over the status of a worker. It helps protect you against lawsuits by independent contractors who suddenly argue that they're "employees" (for instance, in order to bring a discrimination case or qualify for stock options and retirement benefits). And it's a chance to spell out who owns the work you're requesting *(see Q21).*

Here are some points to cover:

◆ Describe the work you're having done.

◆ Say how you'll pay for it (by the hour or, better yet, by the project).

◆ Mention that the consultant is performing the services as an independent contractor of your company, not as an employee.

◆ Give the starting and ending date of the agreement. Making the contract less than a year long will help avoid suggestions that the consultant is your employee; you can always renew the contract if the work takes longer than that.

◆ Specify how either of you may terminate the agreement and how much notice you each must give each other.

◆ Describe which expenses, if any, you will reimburse.

◆ Define trade secrets and require that the consultant not disclose them *(see Q31).* Or include a broader provision that the consultant may not reveal anything about the work to people outside your company.

◆ Say who owns the copyright to the work being done *(see Q21).*

TIP: Depending on the complexity of your relationship with the consultant, the first draft of the agreement may be just a starting point for negotiations. Unless you have a lot of experience with these contracts, it's best to have your lawyer review this document before you sign on the dotted line.

FYI: You can find sample forms (hard copy and a computer disk) with instructions about adapting them to your own needs in the book *Hiring Independent Contractors: The Employer's Legal Guide*, by Stephen Fishman (Nolo Press, $29.95).

SHOULD I PUT JOB AGREEMENTS IN WRITING?

Q 57 THIS IS ONE OF THE RARE INSTANCES IN business when you might be better off without a contract. That's because of a legal doctrine called "employment at will." This rule, which prevails in most states, says that you can usually fire a worker for any reason, as long as it doesn't break a contract or a law (such as those that prohibit discrimination based on sex, race, religion, nationality, age, or disability).

A contract could force you to come up with a better justification—"termination for cause" as lawyers say. Since most employment contracts favor workers, it's not usually enough that someone was doing a bad job, says Robert J. Reicher, an attorney in New York City. More typically the worker must do something wrong, like disobeying orders or purposely harming the company.

Keep in mind that a "contract" doesn't have to be a formal document. A simple exchange of letters confirming a job offer could pin you to obligations you'd rather not have. If you must put that job offer in writing, stick to the basics, like salary and starting date. Avoid saying how long the employment will last or suggesting that the arrangement can't be terminated.

When the person you're hiring has enough leverage to demand a written agreement, Reicher suggests you keep it brief. Here are some key points to think about:

♦ **Term.** The contract should say exactly how long it lasts and how to renew it. Employees usually want a longer contract. A fair compromise is to agree on a shorter term (say three years), giving you an option to extend (perhaps for another two) when the initial term is up.

◆ **Salary, raises, and bonuses.** It's okay to give a starting salary, but after that leave bonuses and salary increases entirely up to you.

◆ **Assignments of patents and copyrights.** If you're in a creative business, such a provision eliminates any uncertainty that might otherwise arise about who owns intellectual property that stems from an employee's work *(see Q21)*.

◆ **"Cause" for termination.** You'll want it as broad as possible, since when you fire someone for cause, you owe them next to nothing. Certain buzzwords give you a lot of wiggle room: "in the company's discretion," "at the company's option," "for any reason," or "at any time."

If you have a written contract and fire someone without cause, you could get stuck paying that person's salary for whatever time they have left in the contract. Fortunately, the law automatically imposes a "duty to mitigate"—an obligation to look for another job. When that happens, the money a worker earns there gets subtracted from what you owe. For example: someone earning $50,000 a year who's fired with one year left in the contract and accepts another job for $30,000, would get $20,000 from the former employer ($50,000 minus $30,000).

Some lawyers representing workers ask for a contract provision relieving their clients of the duty to mitigate. The net result could be a windfall for the person you fired. In negotiating job agreements, therefore, you'll want to stick to your guns.

Setting House Rules

WITHIN THE LIMITS OF WHAT THE LAW PERMITS, YOU MAKE the rules that apply to your business. Even if your shop seems too small to have formal standards, it's important to let staff know what's expected of them. And once you set those rules, be sure to apply them evenhandedly, so you won't be accused of discrimination.

WHAT RULES APPLY UNDER THE FAMILY AND MEDICAL LEAVE ACT?

 THE FEDERAL FAMILY AND MEDICAL LEAVE ACT, or FMLA, requires many businesses to give workers up to 12 weeks per year of family or medical leave for health emergencies or the arrival of a child.

Companies affected generally have 50 or more employees at or near any given work site. Employees need not be paid during such leaves, but they are entitled to continued health benefits with the business paying its share of the premium, and they have the right to return to a comparable job within the firm.

Under FMLA, firms must permit a worker to take a leave in connection with the birth or adoption of a child or placement of a foster child with the employee. Extended absences, as well as reduced schedules and intermittent leaves (such as one day a week on a continuing basis), are permitted when: an employee's "serious health condition" makes it impossible for him or her to do the job or the individual needs to care for a spouse, parent, or child with such a problem.

The law broadly defines "serious health condition" as an "illness, injury, impairment, or physical or mental condition" that requires inpatient or outpatient medical care. Employers may require proof of the medical problem, whether the illness involves a worker or that person's family.

To be eligible for leave, an individual must have been with the company for at least a year and have worked at least 1,250 hours during that period. If a company has fewer than 50 employees at a work site or within a 75-mile radius of that site, it may deny the leave. In companies that would otherwise be subject to the law, owners can also exempt from coverage certain highly paid employees whose absence would cause economic harm to the company. In either of these cases, the company is under no obligation to continue a worker's health benefits during a leave or guarantee them a job when they return.

Particularly troublesome for many small businesses is the

obligation under federal law to provide most employees coming back from leave with the same position or one that's equivalent to the job held previously. To get a staffer's work done during his or her absence, a company may fill the position on a temporary basis or require other workers to pitch in. If a firm hires a permanent replacement, however, it must be sure there is another comparable job available when the employee returns.

TIP: Consider publishing a leave policy if you don't already have one. If you do, have an employment lawyer review it to make sure it is consistent with the law. To help you deal with absences that may occur, you can include in your policy a request that employees give you 30 days' notice of the leave.

FYI: A free booklet, *The Family and Medical Leave Act of 1993 (WH Publication 1419)*, is available from the U.S. Labor Department Wage and Hour Division (check the Blue Pages of the local phone book for the one nearest you). Included in the booklet is a copy of the law, extensive regulations explaining the ins and outs of how it's applied, and a sample form that companies can use to respond to workers' requests for leave.

FYI: Failure by a company to comply with the requirements of the law could lead to claims by employees or by the U.S. Department of Labor. If the firm loses, the court could order it to pay monetary damages to workers. At least a dozen states and the District of Columbia have family-leave laws that may impose additional requirements and remedies.

SHOULD I REQUIRE ARBITRATION OF EMPLOYMENT DISPUTES?

 THIS IS CURRENTLY ONE OF THE MOST DIVISIVE issues in employment law. The controversy surrounds what are known as predispute arbitration clauses: agreements made long before any trouble arises that workers will use arbitration to resolve disputes with the company.

In most arbitrations, the case goes before an arbitrator or a panel of three. Usually their decision is binding and can't be appealed. Unlike lawsuits, which can take years to thrash out in court, arbitration has at least the potential of resolving things in a matter of days or weeks. It also keeps cases away from juries, many of whom are working people and see things from the employee's perspective.

While this conflict resolution technique may be appropriate in certain cases *(see Q97)*, there are inherent problems with predispute arbitration clauses. Some companies require workers to sign them as early as on the job application, or later when bonuses, stock options, or promotions are awarded. The net effect is that workers lose the right to a jury trial—a right guaranteed by certain laws, including the federal Civil Rights Act and the Americans with Disabilities Act *(see Q51)*. On these and other grounds, predispute arbitration clauses have faced widespread court challenges in recent years.

By making arbitration mandatory, companies cause employees to become suspicious of the process and more likely to challenge it in court. There are better ways to keep disputes out of court than forcing workers to decide ahead of time how to resolve conflicts.

One option is mediation, in which you and the worker negotiate a mutually acceptable settlement rather than having one imposed on you by an arbitrator *(see Q97)*. Mediation can prevent further damage to work relationships if an employee is still at the company. This confidential method also works well when there are sensitive issues that could prove embarrassing to both employee and company—as there are in sexual harassment cases *(see Q68)*. "Accommodation" cases under the Americans with Disabilities Act *(see Q51)* are also good candidates for mediation, since it can lead to creative solutions.

Another possibility is a multistep approach, such as informal discussion between the worker and management, followed by mediation with the help of a neutral third party. If these methods fail, voluntary resolution by an outside arbitrator could be the final option.

DO I NEED A COMPANY HANDBOOK FOR LEGAL REASONS?

Q 60 IT'S IRONIC THAT THIS DOCUMENT, MEANT TO offer legal protections, has generated so much litigation. Much of it centers on the question of whether the handbook creates a contract, limiting a company's ability to hire and fire "at will" *(see Q57)*.

That said, a handbook has distinct advantages. It collects within one document all the policies and protocols you might otherwise issue separately. Many small-business owners think giving out a handbook sounds far too formal, but having one can help your case if you're slapped with an employment lawsuit: in court, the handbook serves as evidence that you let workers know what to expect.

Law firms charge a hefty premium ($2,000 or $3,000) to pull together their own "kitchen-tested" clauses and tailor them to your needs. The alternative is to cut and paste your own, borrowing language from other businesses, computer software, and on-line material *(see FYI)*. If you go this low-budget route, it's important to have a lawyer review the draft for hidden traps. The $1,000 or so that you'll need to spend (for four or five hours of an attorney's time) could save you a bundle in the long run.

Your handbook doesn't need to be a bulky text written in legalese. In fact, this is one case where, both from a legal perspective and as a matter of employee relations, less is usually more. Here are the basics:

◆ **Employment status.** You'll want to define part-time and full-time employees, indicate who's entitled to benefits, and say what those benefits are.

◆ **Workers' rights.** This is the place to indicate that you don't discriminate in hiring, firing, or promotions and to weave in your sexual harassment policy *(see Q68)*. You should also put workers on notice about their rights to family and medical leave *(see Q58)* and overtime *(see Q61–62)*.

◆ **Company rules.** These are the policies that you must apply to all workers. Depending on your business, they might cover:

— attendance

- behavior toward customers and other employees
- nepotism *(see Q53)*
- drug testing *(see Q52)*
- moonlighting *(see Q63)*
- confidentiality *(see Q31)*
- use of business equipment *(see Q65–67)*
- patents and copyrights *(see Q21)*
- dispute resolution.

◆ **Disclaimer.** Your handbook should indicate that it is not a contract and reserve your right to fire employees at any time, for any reason, with or without cause. This "disclaimer" ought to be written in plain English—not legalese—so all employees can understand it. Be sure that the disclaimer doesn't contradict other provisions, such as those about firing and discipline. Include the disclaimer in these sections, and conspicuously place it near the front of the manual (preferably on its own page).

◆ **Receipt.** Lest your handbook languish in a drawer, you should give workers a couple of days to look it over, then ask them to sign a statement that they have read the document, understand it, and agree to be bound by your rules. Issue and collect a similar receipt any time you make changes in the handbook.

FYI: Given the amount of litigation surrounding employee handbooks, it's best not to prepare these documents completely alone. If you'd like to cut costs by doing some of the drafting, here are materials you may find helpful.

Within CourtTV's Law Center (http://www.courttv.com), a law-related Internet site, is a Small Business Law Center that covers the topic of employee handbooks. Check the "Forms and Model Documents" area, which has a handbook outline prepared by a reputable law firm. The "Seminar and Discussion" area includes the transcript of an on-line "seminar" called "The Ultimate Employee Handbook" workshop, which offers sample language.

Employee Manual Maker is a handbook template that business owners can adapt to their own use. It comes in book version, with the same text on diskette, and covers more territory than most small-business owners need to consider. The package costs $139 and is available from Jian at 800-440-5426.

WHO'S ENTITLED TO OVERTIME PAY?

 UNDER THE FAIR LABOR STANDARDS ACT, HOURLY employees (who tend to be blue-collar workers) are entitled to overtime pay—at least time and a half—if they work more than 40 hours in a week.

Salaried workers, on the other hand, are exempt from overtime pay requirements. Labor Department regulations describe these employees as people who hold executive, administrative, or professional positions and are guaranteed a salary of at least $250 per week, regardless of the number of hours they work.

However, in recent years the Department of Labor has said that regardless of whether employees otherwise meet the definition, they cannot be considered salaried if company policies or practices permit pay deductions for partial-day absences. If these policies exist, the agency argues, even workers whom a company calls "salaried" must be paid overtime.

The safest bet is not docking salaried employees for partial-day absences, says Samuel D. Walker, a lawyer with Wiley, Rein & Fielding in Washington, D.C. Instead, many companies create a leave bank or allotment of personal days that workers can draw upon. Most courts have said it's okay to debit partial-day absences against these accounts. But you might run afoul of the rules if you require someone to use up a full day of leave for a partial day's absence.

What happens when the leave bank or personal days are used up? Again, you can't dock salaried employees for part of a day, Walker says. But if they're chronically absent (or late), and it's not for medical reasons (*see Q51, Q58*), you can fire them for poor attendance.

TIP: Review your company's written pay policy. It should clearly say that salaried workers cannot have pay deducted for partial-day absences.

SMALL BUSINESS LEGAL SMARTS

HIRING AND MANAGING EMPLOYEES

FYI: Outside the scope of the federal overtime rule are partial days off that employers must permit under the federal Family and Medical Leave Act *(see Q58)*. Still, that law applies only to a narrow range of cases, such as those involving serious health conditions of employees or their families and the birth or adoption of children.

CAN I OFFER EMPLOYEES A CHOICE BETWEEN COMPENSATORY AND OVERTIME PAY?

 NOT IF THEY'RE COVERED BY FEDERAL REGULA-tions on hourly workers. Most often these "non-exempt" employees are blue collar workers or those who don't hold managerial, administrative, or executive positions. The law requires that these employees be paid overtime if they work more than 40 hours in a week *(see Q61)*. You may not offer them time off instead.

That's true even if the employee requests time off in writing. The federal government fears a boss could force workers to sign statements claiming they'd rather get comp time.

CAN I PREVENT STAFF FROM MOONLIGHTING?

 IT'S PERFECTLY LEGAL TO REQUIRE EMPLOYEES not to moonlight as a condition of working at your company. And you can usually fire a worker for any reason, as long as it doesn't break a contract or a law *(see Q57)*. If you're worried about moonlighting, however, it's best to make your position clear, whether you prohibit it altogether or just require workers to get your approval first.

Before you do, though, think through the pros and cons of such a policy. Many businesses have permitted employees to teach evening courses at local schools, figuring it's good publicity and helps recruit new hires. Others actually tutor staff about self-employment, anticipating that these workers may soon be laid off and come back to work as freelancers. Allowing moonlighting is also a way to at least temporarily hold on to good help when you can't afford to pay them quite what they're worth.

The downside, for companies looking to get the maximum work out of the fewest people, is that moonlighting is a distraction. You don't want workers turning you down for overtime because they have to dash off to work a second shift someplace else. You don't want them showing up drowsy because they've been up half the night freelancing. And you certainly don't want them jumping ship the minute their enterprise gets off the ground.

Divided loyalties are another problem. Some workers may be tempted to do outside work on your time or compete for customers. There are also situations in which work from one job (including access to confidential information) interferes with a worker's ability to be fair or honest in the other.

If your staff members are running a competing business, the law in most states permits you to fire them. Otherwise the best approach is to treat the moonlighting as a performance issue. If there has been no deterioration in someone's work, you should probably just monitor the situation and let the employee credit you with being a terrific boss.

If the sideline business results in, say, repeated lateness or reduced productivity, you should take steps to improve the situation. Meet with the employee and explain your objections. Give him or her a chance to improve (from two weeks to several months, depending on the extent of the problem), and follow up with a clear written warning ("You will be fired if you continue to miss project deadlines," for example). Should you dismiss workers who have been moonlighting, let them know that you are doing so because they have fallen short on the job.

TIP: Some small companies set themselves up for problems by allowing flexible hours. That gives people time to do something else, whether it's taking care of kids or working another job.

Managing Within the Law

WORKERS ARE INCREASINGLY SAVVY ABOUT THEIR ON-THE-JOB rights. Business owners need to be at least as well informed. A company that underestimates what employees know about the law of the workplace does so at its peril.

DO ANTIDISCRIMINATION LAWS APPLY TO PROMOTIONS?

 ABSOLUTELY. THESE INCLUDE FEDERAL LAWS prohibiting discrimination on the basis of race, sex, national origin, age, and disability as well as local laws that (depending on the state) may protect employees from bias linked to sexual orientation or marital status.

If a court finds your action discriminatory, it could order you to give the next available promotion to the employee who brought suit and to make up for lost wages and pension benefits. Some states permit recovery of damages for emotional distress.

Even subtle action may be discriminatory. For instance, it may be illegal to use standards, such as educational requirements, that apply to everyone but put a particular group at a unique disadvantage unless such standards are directly related to the job. Your tendency to promote people whom you like may also discriminate against other qualified individuals, says Helene M. Freeman of Dorsey & Whitney. "Sometimes bosses are unaware of their biases," she adds. "They may assume, for example, that single workers and married women don't need promotions and that older employees don't deserve them because their utility is limited."

123

TIP: To avoid charges of discrimination, use memos or bulletin board notices to invite your staff to apply for positions that open up. Give thorough descriptions of the jobs, as well as lists of any qualifications you require; if you demand a certain level of education, be sure it is necessary for the job. Make clear that you plan to base your selection solely on merit. As you make your decision, remember: you may someday be asked to explain your choice.

DO EMPLOYEES GENERALLY HAVE A RIGHT TO PRIVACY?

THERE'S NO FEDERAL LAW THAT COVERS ALL aspects of a person's right to privacy. To date, a patchwork of state laws prohibits eavesdropping (see Q66), drug testing (see Q52), and other forms of privacy invasion by employers within those state borders.

For example, employers generally have the right to search desks, file cabinets, and offices since it's assumed they are provided for business use. In contrast, most courts have found that employees have the right to expect that they won't be snooped on in lavatories, lockers, and to a lesser extent, lunchrooms and lounges, which are considered private and for their personal use. The proliferation of leading-edge technologies has intensified concerns over the boundaries between permissible monitoring and illegal snooping.

You stand a greater chance of defending your use of potentially intrusive searches if you have a valid business purpose for conducting them in the first place. For example, you might be able to search a locker to maintain a drug-free workplace, listen in on telephone calls to conduct performance reviews, and read faxes to prevent unauthorized use of your company's equipment.

Theoretically, you can use video monitors and phone bugs to serve a legitimate business purpose, such as checking up on an employee suspected of theft. But even then, the act of videotaping may prompt a lawsuit, especially when it takes place in an area like a locker room, which many employees presume is private.

How much privacy your employees can expect also depends a lot on your policies or practices. If your company handbook *(see Q60)* makes specific references to "employees' desks," for instance, you could create a right of privacy where a court might not otherwise find one. By the same reasoning, an employee who gives his supervisor the combination to his locker might negate any expectations about privacy that would ordinarily apply.

You can outline your expectations—and reduce the risk of privacy lawsuits—by letting employees know in advance that you intend to monitor their activities. That way you both know what to expect, and a court will probably say employees consented to your actions.

The most comprehensive approach is to remind employees, via memo, policy statement, or handbook *(see Q60)* that company property—for instance, desks, file cabinets, fax machines, e-mail, or voice mail—is provided for business use. This way, you reserve the right to inspect property and monitor communication *(see Q66–67)* for whatever business purpose you may later identify, whether it involves tracking down drug dealing or misuse of trade secrets *(see Q30)*.

TIP: It's a good idea to have your lawyer review your policies and check the laws of your state. To make sure employees know the ground rules, have them sign a statement that they've read and understand them.

IS IT LEGAL TO LISTEN IN ON EMPLOYEES' PHONE CALLS?

Q 66 LISTENING TO BUSINESS-RELATED TELEPHONE calls made to and from the company is one of the most common forms of workplace monitoring. Companies dependent on extensive telephone work—such as telemarketers and insurance companies—often listen in to evaluate the success of their training and improve customer service. Other companies, trying to cut costs, listen in on staffers to make sure they're not using the phones for excessive personal calls.

A federal law, referred to as "the wiretap law," permits employers to listen to employees' calls "in the ordinary course of business." Some states specifically require that employees be notified of the practice ahead of time. That's a good preventive measure even if your state doesn't require advance notice.

Deciding what to do with the information you collect is a trickier matter. Suppose that while collecting information about illegal gambling, you overhear an employee talking with his psychiatrist. If, in this case, the material serves no business purpose, destroy it. If you uncover criminal behavior, turn it over to law enforcement authorities.

The line between snooping and acceptable monitoring becomes even blurrier when you discover misconduct other than what you were looking for. Let's say, for example, that you were listening in to monitor excessive personal use of the company phone and found that a worker was goofing off or passing trade secrets to a competitor. In that event, inform the employee of your findings and take disciplinary action. To keep a potentially dicey situation from escalating into a privacy lawsuit, try to avoid Draconian measures like termination.

WHEN CAN I READ WORKERS' COMPUTER-TO-COMPUTER MESSAGES?

Q 67 MOST PRIVACY LAWSUITS ARISE BECAUSE employees expect messages they send to be private but find out they aren't. If you don't want employees using computers, networks, and Internet connections for personal matters, be sure to distribute rules that they're only for business use. You can remind them of your policy each time they sign on by programming the system to display a message reiterating these rules.

A more lenient and employee-friendly alternative would be creating bulletin boards that employees can use to send personal messages or passwords that allow them to protect those messages. Passwords can also be used to protect some voice-mail messages. If you permit employees to send personal messages, be sure to retain the right to intercept them when you have to repair or maintain the telephone or computer equipment. That warning also puts employees on notice that their privacy is not guaranteed.

FYI: *Privacy Tool Kit* supplies sample e-mail policies that companies can adapt. Written by David R. Johnson, an attorney, and John Podesta, a consultant, this 42-page guide includes answers to some commonly asked questions as well as tips for formulating e-mail policies. It is available from the Electronic Messaging Association at 703-524-5550 and costs $20 for members and $45 for nonmembers.

AM I LIABLE FOR SEXUAL HARASSMENT CAUSED BY OTHER PEOPLE?

Q 68 YES. COURTS ARE INCREASINGLY SYMPATHETIC to sexual harassment charges and have held owners responsible for the actions of an employee's supervisors, co-workers, and even outside parties who deal with the company, such as vendors and customers. In cases of one co-worker harassing another, owners are liable if they knew or should have known about the harassment and didn't take prompt remedial action. It's therefore important that supervisors and middle managers understand exactly what sexual harassment is and be prepared to respond to a grievance.

Guidelines issued by the U.S. Equal Employment Opportunity Commission define sexual harassment as "unwelcome" sexual behavior. The most blatant form involves a "quid pro quo": explicitly or implicitly offering a benefit, such as a raise or promotion, in exchange for sex. But the EEOC guidelines also prohibit more subtle sexual behavior that makes the workplace a "hostile or offensive environment." This might include making lewd jokes, posting obscene photographs, or touching. The Supreme Court ruled in 1998 that harassment includes not only behavior by members of the opposite sex but also by members of the same sex.

The best way to avoid liability is to try and stop sexual harassment before it starts by prohibiting it in an employee handbook *(see Q60)* or written policy statement. Addressing sexual harassment in writing serves a number of purposes. It notifies workers that sexual harassment is unacceptable, thereby helping to deter such conduct. It lets employees know how and where they can complain about a problem, increasing the odds that offensive behavior will be reported and that the company owners will be able to take prompt remedial action. In case of a lawsuit, the existence of a policy may also reduce the employer's liability if, for example, the employee failed to complain through company channels, or if the employer has responded with prompt remedial action when the person did complain.

Preparing a policy doesn't have to be expensive. One option is showing an employment lawyer the sample wording in this book *(see box on page 128)* and asking whether he or she can tailor it to your business. The policy you adopt should inform workers that sexual harassment will not be tolerated, give them examples of the type of conduct that will be characterized as sexual harassment, and create a channel though which staffers can make a complaint without fear of retaliation.

Sample Sexual Harassment Policy

IT IS [NAME OF YOUR COMPANY] policy to prohibit harassment of
one employee by another employee, supervisor, or third party
(including vendors, suppliers, or customers) on the basis of sex.
While it is not easy to define precisely what harassment
is, it certainly includes unwelcome jokes, innuendos or comments, sexual advances, requests for sexual favors,
unwanted touching, sexually related postings or pictures,
and other verbal, visual, or physical conduct of a sexual
nature. Any employee who feels that he or she has been sub-
jected to sexual harassment should immediately report the
matter to [supervisor], or [human resource person, if any],
or [company president]. Violations of this policy will not be
permitted and will result in disciplinary action up to and
including discharge. Employees can be assured that no one
will be retaliated against for either filing a complaint or
participating in an investigation of harassment.

SOURCE: REPRINTED WITH PERMISSION OF THE LAW FIRM JACKSON, LEWIS, SCHNITZLER & KRUPMAN

128

It's also important to offer employees more than one person to report incidents to, so they're not forced to bring their
grievances to the very individual who has been harassing
them. In a small company, investigations can be run by a manager, a supervisor, or the company owner *(see Q69)*.

Your sexual harassment policy can be incorporated into
your employee handbook *(see Q60)*, if you have one, and
should also be distributed to your employees as a separate
document. Find occasions to call it to the attention of your
workers: for example, discuss it during orientation of new
employees, when promotions occur, or at staff meetings.

HOW SHOULD I RESPOND TO SEXUAL HARASSMENT COMPLAINTS?

 69 IT'S THE RESPONSIBILITY OF THE COMPANY,
through a manager or a supervisor, to immediately
meet with those who've complained and get the full
story. During this meeting, find out how the events affected
employees' ability to do their jobs. For example, are they

afraid to walk though the parking lot or embarrassed to enter the employee lunchroom? Do they dread coming to work?

Ask whether the employee feels he or she has been singled out for the abuse and whether any other workers have been harassed by the same person. In the course of your discussion, you may discover that other staff members have experienced the problem, witnessed it, or know about it.

Here are some sample questions you should ask when meeting with an employee who has complained about sexual harassment:

◆ What happened?
◆ How often has this occurred?
◆ What was the sequence of events?
◆ Did you in any way consent to the behavior?
◆ How have you responded to the person who harassed you?
◆ Did anyone else see or hear what happened to you?
◆ Has [the accused] punished you in any way?
◆ Have you told anybody about your problems with [the accused]?
◆ Have any other employees mentioned to you that they've experienced a similar problem with [the accused]?
◆ Are there any documents or is there any other evidence involved?
◆ How does this conduct make you feel?
◆ What effect, if any, has this behavior had on your ability to do your job?

It's important that your investigation not intimidate the person who has complained or take on the tone of an inquisition. Even if you'd like to tape the interview or get a signed complaint, you can't require either. And just raising the subject could cause people to clam up. A better option is to take copious notes during the interview and review them with the employee in the meeting.

Once you've heard the complaint, investigate it right away (within a day for a simple matter; no more than a week for a complex situation). Gather whatever additional information you need to evaluate the claim. If there is tangible evidence, such as pornographic magazines or pinups, collect the items. Speak to any witnesses or other employees who may also have been harassed.

If the victim does not provide the names of other workers who may be affected, conduct a confidential, informal survey. Speak with your employees individually. Tell them the company has a policy against sexual harassment and ask them whether they've ever had such a problem. Again, be careful not to pressure people or point the finger: you can't punish staff for refusing to cooperate.

Your next step is to hear the other side of the story. Privately inform accused parties of the charges and give them a chance to answer them. If they want to speak to a lawyer first, by all means let them, but you're under no obligation to inform people of any rights before they answer your questions. Nor is it necessary to identify the complainant, although the accused will probably know, or guess, who made the charge. Tell any accused people that they should not confront their accusers or retaliate in any way and that if they do, you will consider that insubordination and take appropriate action.

Should you conclude that sexual harassment has occurred, punish the offenders.

For *employees,* you'll want to consider the following factors: the seriousness of the offense, the employee's work record (both in terms of similar prior behavior and overall performance), and how clear it was beforehand that the conduct was unacceptable at your workplace. If the victim has been tangibly harmed (by being denied a pay increase or being fired, let's say), consider how you can repair the damage.

If the accused is a *vendor* or *service person,* get statements from the employees affected and then talk to the individual they have accused. Let the accused know that what's going on is interfering with your employees' well-being and that corrective measures must be taken; if the behavior doesn't stop, take your business elsewhere.

Clients or *customers* who harass your staff members are more difficult. Sometimes you have the option of assigning a different employee to the department or account. However, removing the victim from the situation must not damage, or appear to damage, the staffer's career. Merely replacing the target of the harassment can also send a message to the client that you don't object to the harassment.

TIP: Maintain confidentiality during the investigation and, if harassment is confirmed, while disciplining the perpetrator. Without confidentiality, the facts of what occurred may get exaggerated, and people may be afraid to participate in your investigation. You also increase the risk of a defamation claim being brought by the person who is accused of the objectionable behavior.

TIP: Law firms and nonlawyer consultants are widely available to privately investigate sexual harassment on the job. But unless you don't have the time or inclination to handle these issues yourself, a small company probably won't need them to lead the investigation. Do call an employment lawyer if workers suddenly bring in theirs or you have any questions along the way.

Parting Company

FIRING A WORKER WHOM YOU'VE COME TO KNOW AND MAY like on a personal level can be a painful and difficult task. Increasingly that already thorny chore is compounded by the possibility that the employee will bring a lawsuit against you and your business. How you part ways can make the difference between workers who quietly move on to new positions and those who take their anger to court.

HOW CAN I STOP A FIRING FROM BACKFIRING?

 HERE ARE 10 STEPS YOU CAN TAKE TO MINIMIZE that risk and come out on the winning side if you're sued.

1 **Give a valid reason for the firing.** Trimming staff and eliminating jobs are good ways to justify a dismissal. Just be sure the circumstances don't suggest you have other motives for the discharge, like replacing a highly paid worker with a younger one who earns substantially less money.

For performance problems, the key is to be as concrete as possible in expressing your objections, whether they relate to insubordination, causing morale problems, or misrepresenting the company.

2 **Brief employees on their shortcomings.** Unless the situation involves theft, destruction of property or safety concerns, immediate dismissal for poor performance isn't a good idea legally or managerially. Instead, meet with the employee face to face and explain the problem. To prevent misunderstandings, you might want to have a witness present, such as your second in command or a manager.

Be firm. For example, you might say: "We've had our biggest client tell us that you don't return phone calls promptly and have been late to meetings. We pride ourselves on our service and think it's important that you be more attentive to this client's needs. Unless you address these complaints to our satisfaction, we will have to let you go."

3 **Give employees a chance to correct the problem.** Warning employees and giving them an opportunity to improve will strengthen your case, since it shows that you've been fair and documents your objections before the firing. The time between a warning and a dismissal can be anywhere from two weeks to several months and will depend on the employee's job and the seriousness of the problem.

4 **Document verbal warnings.** After each meeting with the employee, write a memo to your file clearly explaining your concerns. Be sure your notes show that you gave the employee a chance to improve. Don't crowd your file with memos written during the last few days before you fire an employee, however. It looks as if you're trumping up complaints to justify getting rid of somebody.

5 **Follow up with a written warning.** A written warning is evidence that you told the employee about the problem. It should be clear and direct: "Your job is in jeopardy." Avoid vague phrases like "If you fail to correct this problem further action will be taken," since employees could later argue that they expected another warning. Ask the employee to sign the warning.

6 **Watch your language.** When you speak to the employee in person and follow up with written warnings, be careful to say

nothing that could be interpreted even loosely as discriminatory. "She doesn't project the proper image for our company"
might later be interpreted as a sexist or racist remark. "We
wanted to do things a new way and John couldn't adapt,"
might be construed as age discrimination. So could a casual
remark like "you've been around here a long time."

7 **Seek an "independent review" of the firing decision.**
Ask a third party, such as a co-owner or another supervisor,
to review all aspects of the case before you actually fire the
employee. Don't rely on a lawyer for this task, since it looks
as though you're preparing for litigation.

8 **Be humane when you do the firing.** Aim for a 10-minute,
face-to-face meeting in which you quickly tell the employee
exactly why you're firing him or her, set a prompt departure
date, and explain the terms of the severance package.

If you're dealing with a question of fact, get the employee's
side of the story and write it down. Creating an atmosphere
of evenhandedness, if not compassion, goes a long way
toward keeping an employee from feeling vengeful and seek-
ing redress through the courts.

9 **Ask the employee for a release.** If you think the departing
staff member will sue, you may want to offer the person
extra severance pay in exchange for a waiver (a release from
legal claims). To withstand a court challenge from a former
employee, a waiver must be voluntary. In exchange for the
agreement, you must have given the worker "consideration,"
that is, some kind of monetary bonus that's more than he or
she would have been entitled to under the regular severance
package. Benefits linked to waivers may include cash payments, credits toward a pension plan, and continuation of
paid medical benefits. The waiver should also include a confidentiality provision prohibiting the departing employee
from discussing severance terms.

For workers older than 40, who are protected against age
discrimination, federal law imposes extra requirements
before a waiver will be considered valid. You must advise
employees in writing to see a lawyer before signing the
agreement and give them least 21 days to decide whether to
sign (45 days if you're firing more than one person at a time).

In addition, the release must:

◆ Be written in plain English
◆ Say that workers are relinquishing their right to sue under the Age Discrimination in Employment Act
◆ Offer people at least seven days to change their minds.

10 Don't hinder the employee's job search. If prospective employers inquire, be careful: bad references can invite a libel suit; good references, however, can backfire, since they might suggest there was no reason to fire the employee. Instead, simply confirm the dates of employment and the job title.

WHEN MUST I CONTINUE HEALTH BENEFITS FOR EX-EMPLOYEES?

Q 71 THE FEDERAL COBRA (CONSOLIDATED OMNIBUS Budget Reconciliation Act) law requires most companies with 20 or more employees to continue group health coverage for former employees for at least 18 months after they've left their jobs, unless they become covered by another employer's group health plan (one that doesn't exclude or limit coverage for a preexisting condition) during that period. Former employees must pay the cost of coverage (whatever you spend to cover a worker) plus a small fee for administrative expenses. Failure to comply with COBRA obligations could lead to a lawsuit by employees, their beneficiaries, or the U.S. Department of Labor, as well as a variety of monetary penalties imposed by the courts or the IRS. Many states have COBRA-like laws that may impose additional requirements on business owners.

Employers can get into trouble by failing to notify employees of their COBRA rights, says Paul Hamburger, an attorney with McDermott, Will & Emery in Washington, D.C. A company's precise obligations and the time during which they apply will depend on whether the firm or its insurance carrier administers the health plan. If your insurer is the administrator, you have 30 days to let the insurer know that the employee has left the job, and the insurer has 14 more days to notify the employee. Check your policy, though: it's not unusual for a carrier, regardless of its role in paying claims, to list the employer as the plan administrator. In that case, you technically have 44 days from the date employees leave your firm to inform them of their COBRA rights; however, you should notify workers as soon as possible, to avoid charges that you failed to give them ample notice.

You also must supply COBRA notice in cases of other "qualifying events," such as the death or divorce of the employee (because the employee's spouse and dependent children are entitled to COBRA) and when a child ceases to be a dependent. Whatever the qualifying events, the COBRA notices must give employees and their families at least 60 days (from either the date of the notice or the date coverage would otherwise stop, whichever is later) to elect coverage. Keep copies of all notices, along with records of the qualifying events, when the elections were made, and any payments that were received. You can satisfy COBRA requirements by sending the notice by first-class mail to the employee's last known address. But for documentation purposes you might prefer certified mail.

WHAT ARE THE REQUIREMENTS FOR MY HEALTH INSURANCE PLAN?

 A 1996 LAW, KNOWN AS THE HEALTH INSURANCE Portability and Accountability Act, or HIPAA, makes it easier for workers to continue coverage when they move from one job to the next. The law, which applies to all health insurance plans that cover two or more current employees, creates a number of administrative burdens for companies. Here are some steps to take:

◆ **Be sure your plan permits coverage for "preexisting conditions."** One of the key changes of this law was to create a nationwide standard for "preexisting conditions." You'll want to revise your plan to be sure it conforms with these rules.

The law says that new employees (and their spouses and children) can't be permanently closed out of a company's plan just because of a preexisting condition. Definition: a physical or mental condition "for which medical advice, diagnosis, care, or treatment was recommended or received" within six months of enrolling in your company's plan.

You can delay coverage for a preexisting condition for up to 12 months (18 months in some cases). For people who had health insurance before joining the company (for instance, if they were covered under a spouse's plan or had an individual policy), the waiting period gets shortened by the number of months they had coverage.

Things get tricky if employees have a gap in coverage—let's say because they were out of work for a while and couldn't afford insurance. When that break lasts more than 63 days, the clock gets set back on preexisting conditions. These workers have to wait a year from the date of enrolling in your plan (18 months in some cases) for preexisting conditions to be covered.

◆ **Issue "certificates of coverage."** Because workers' rights under the law depend partly on whatever insurance they had last, they'll need some proof of what the coverage was. To that end, the law requires companies to issue a certificate of coverage whenever someone loses coverage under the plan.

You must supply this certificate no matter why the person has lost coverage—whether they've left the company, or just dropped the insurance during an open enrollment period, says Paul Hamburger. The requirement applies whether the covered person is an employee, spouse, or dependent. If that person continues coverage under COBRA (see Q71), you must issue another certificate when they lose COBRA coverage. You also must issue a certificate to anyone who requests it within 24 months of losing either initial coverage or COBRA coverage.

How soon must you issue the certificates? That depends on the reason for the loss, Hamburger says. If it's because of a COBRA "qualifying event" (see Q71), you have as long as you'd have under COBRA—generally 14 days after the plan administrator is notified of the coverage loss. Otherwise, the law isn't clear. As a rule, small businesses should send out the certificates within two weeks of being notified of the coverage loss, says Hamburger. Your health insurer can supply a sample certificate.

◆ **Keep careful records.** Starting July 1, 1998, the certificate must include the name of the covered person (who may be a dependent, not necessarily the person on your staff). There-fore, you'll want to get on file the names of all people covered under family plans. Hamburger also suggests you track how long each person has been covered and what they're covered for (such as mental health, prescription drugs, and substance abuse). Keep these records for at least two years after any coverage loss. With these records in hand, preparing the certificate is fairly straightforward. All you'll need to add is the name of the person to contact for more information.

Though you might just rely on your insurer to handle the paperwork, Hamburger advises against that. Both insurers and types of coverage change, he says, leaving employers best equipped to keep track of the information. Using a third-party plan administrator is another option. If you go this route, be sure to get an "indemnity"—an agreement that if the administrator fouls up, it will reimburse you for any liability.

CHAPTER 5

Marketing Products and Services

BUILDING A BETTER MOUSETRAP IS JUST the first step toward running a successful business. Before you congratulate yourself on a job well done, you must attract customers and clients, spell out the terms of your dealings, and meet any obligations the law imposes.

Along the way, you could stumble into any number of legal pitfalls. Take out an ad and competitors may find legal grounds to challenge the content. Use a Website to reach a wider audience and you open yourself to lawsuits in faraway places. Even the government is there telling you what you've done wrong—with rules on everything from price-fixing to mail order sales.

Those customers whose business you worked so hard to win enjoy a number of protections that you must observe. If you formalize your relationship in a written agreement, it too creates obligations.

Marketing Tools

ANY STRATEGY THAT GIVES YOU A COMMERCIAL
advantage leaves you prey to competitors. Some will
try to use the legal system to gain an advantage.

WHAT CAN I SAY IN ADS THAT COMPARE MY PRODUCTS OR SERVICES TO THOSE OF A COMPETITOR?

 THE FIRST QUESTION IS WHETHER YOUR
comparative advertising makes specific
claims that the consumer assumes can be measured
or proven, says Richard A. Kurnit, an attorney with
Frankfurt, Garbus, Klein & Selz in New York City.
Examples: "These pickles are more sour than brand
X;" "We send more travelers annually to Borneo
than any other U.S. tour operator;" or "Our
lawnmower is easier to push than company B's." All
of these claims can be verified by objective criteria,

such as scientific tests, surveys, or demonstrations. Federal regulations require you to have proof that the advertising is true (called "substantiation") before you make the claim.

At the other end of the spectrum are claims that are pure puffery—things that can't be proven or disproven because they're "too general, hyperbolic, or humorous," Kurnit says. Since such claims cannot be substantiated, federal rules requiring you to have proof on hand before advertising do not apply. For example, a court found that the claim, "Our debt collection service is comparable to those of attorneys," was puffery because it could not be proven. The same reasoning would apply to "try it, you'll like it."

IS IT OKAY IN ANY OTHER CONTEXTS TO MENTION ANOTHER COMPANY'S NAME IN MY ADS?

 UNLESS YOU'RE TRYING TO SHOW WHY YOUR product (or service) is better or more economical, it's risky to mention another company's name in your ads without getting an okay first. That's true whether or not the other company is your competitor, says Lewis Rose, an advertising and marketing law specialist with Arent Fox Kintner Plotkin & Kahn in Washington, D.C.

In particular, the law prohibits you from using others' intellectual property *(see Chapter 2)* to confuse prospective purchasers—for instance by making them think you're somehow associated or by mixing up two brands. A key question is what your action does to the market for the other company's product or services, Rose says. Courts will look closely at the use of another company's name that could boost your profits at their expense.

One time you're usually on safe ground naming names: if the company you're mentioning carries your products—as when a store stocks your widgets and your ad tells potential customers where to buy them.

TIP: Be especially careful when doing business on the Internet. Unauthorized hyperlinks to other companies' sites could get you in trouble, as could putting up pictures or text that violate someone else's copyright *(see Q20–21).*

WHAT ARE THE RULES ABOUT FALSE OR MISLEADING ADVERTISING?

 FEDERAL RULES, AND THOSE OF MANY STATES, require that advertising be truthful, accurate, and that you have substantiation *(see Q73)* for any claims you make. Otherwise you may be subject to suits by the Federal Trade Commission (the primary U.S. government agency that regulates advertising), state attorneys general, and your competitors.

Watch out for advertising that is literally true but misleading, warns Jeffrey Edelstein, a lawyer with Hall Dickler Kent Friedman & Wood in New York City. For instance, an ad for an aspirin product that says four out of five doctors recommend it implies that you took a sizable survey. If you only talked to five doctors, the ad would be misleading.

As with comparative advertising, you must be able to support any objective claim that can be verified. It's best to have this documentation on file before placing the ad.

WHAT OTHER COMMON LEGAL PITFALLS SHOULD I LOOK OUT FOR IN ADVERTISING?

THERE ARE SOME DO'S AND DONT'S TO CONSIDER as you think of ways to promote your product or service:

♦ **Don't** imply that someone is sponsoring your product when they're not.

♦ **Don't** offer a product that's so much like your competitor's (or has such a similar name) that consumers could confuse the two.

♦ **Don't** use a person's name or picture without their written permission. Whether or not a person is famous, if they're recognizable in the ad you might run afoul of state privacy laws, says Edelstein. If you're using the name or picture of a celebrity who's died, state law may require permission from that person's estate.

♦ **Do** read the fine print on invoices from any stock photo houses. Have a lawyer review the terms if you're uneasy about them: often they disclaim any privacy or publicity rights, says Edelstein. That means, for example, you may have bought the photographer's permission to use the picture but still need a release from the people shown in the photo.

◆ **Do** make sure you have all the rights you need to use copyrighted material in your ads. Whenever you purchase material (such as photographs or text) from an outside source (for instance, from a stock photo house or freelancer) get a warranty that it's original, that the person or company you're buying it from owns all the rights you want to buy *(see Q21)*, and that they will indemnify you for any legal problems that might arise (for instance, suits for copyright infringement by someone else who claims to own the work).

At a minimum, you'll want an assignment *(see Q21)* or license *(see Q22)* giving you permission to use the work for a particular purpose. Be sure to specify what that purpose is. For example, if your contract with a stock photo house says you can use a picture in national advertising, you don't automatically have the right to put it on your Website, which is accessible worldwide, Edelstein warns.

◆ **Do** make sure your advertising is not even "substantially similar" *(see Q33)* to that of another company. If it is, you might be accused of copyright infringement.

◆ **Do** watch out for the many types of advertising that are highly regulated by federal and state agencies. Examples are: ads targeted at children and those for sweepstakes, contests, automobiles, financial services, food, drugs, and health-related items (like weight-loss products). You'll want a lawyer knowledgeable about the particular rules to review each of these types of advertising.

◆ **Do** play fair. You'll decrease the likelihood of getting sued and increase the chances of getting the case quickly dismissed if you are.

TIP: It could take as little as 15 minutes to have a lawyer review any advertising before you run it. Given the risks, that's a small price to pay.

FYI: Free information about advertising and marketing law is available on the Advertising Law Internet Site, maintained by Arent Fox Kintner Plotkin & Kahn, the Washington, D.C.,

law firm. The address for the site is http://www.webcom.com/
~lewrose/home.html.

WHAT LEGAL ISSUES ARISE WHEN MY COMPANY MARKETS GOODS AND SERVICES ON ITS OWN WEBSITE?

Q 77 ONE OF THE MORE TROUBLESOME—AND unresolved—issues is where you can be sued, says David Bender, an attorney with White & Case in New York City.

At the heart of the matter is a long-standing body of court cases that say companies can be sued anywhere they "transact" business. The question, then, is whether setting up a Website, accessible from anywhere in the world, fits the definition. If it does, you could be forced to defend yourself in some far-flung places.

You reduce the risk considerably the more "passive" you make the Website, lawyers say. That means limiting it to information: a description of what you do and a list of officers' and directors' phone numbers, for example.

For many business owners, though, the allure of the Internet is the prospect of making a site "interactive": giving people the chance to order goods and services with the click of a mouse, for instance. The more you use the site as a sales tool, the more likely you can be sued where people view it.

That in turn could mean you have to comply with a host of state rules, says Daniel T. Brooks, a lawyer with Cadwalader, Wickersham & Taft in Washington, D.C. These include: state sales tax requirements; health codes (such as those that stop you from transporting fresh fruit between certain states); rules on advertising (some states prohibit advertising by lawyers, doctors, and insurance agents, for instance); and even laws about whether it's legal to sell your product (like guns) in the state. For the latest installment on the growing body of cyberlaw, it's best to check with an attorney who's an Internet expert.

TIP: No matter how careful you are, there's always at least a minimal chance of a lawsuit. When you market on the Internet, you exacerbate any legal pitfalls by extending your reach into so many more jurisdictions.

TIP: If you think an active Website can really boost your sales, it might be worth exposing yourself to the liability that goes with it. Otherwise, you could opt for a more passive site until the law catches up with technology.

WHAT ARE THE COPYRIGHT RISKS OF PUTTING MY MATERIAL ON THE INTERNET?

Q 78 IN AN EFFORT TO PROMOTE THEIR SERVICES OR market products, many businesses are posting written material and making samples available on their Websites. Doing that poses two risks, David Bender says. The first is that people will pirate your material (such as software) instead of buying it. The other is that they'll use what you post for competitive purposes, distributing it to others without paying you or giving you credit. Both problems can be difficult to police.

Before making too much available, it's best to weigh the potential revenues you'll generate through this marketing tool against the risk of having your material ripped off. For whatever you decide to post, here are some precautions to consider:

◆ Include a copyright notice *(see Q20)* on the screen. Though not legally required, it stops infringers from being able to argue that they didn't know you owned the copyright (the "innocent infringer" defense).

◆ Require people to pay (by typing in a credit card number) before downloading anything from your site.

◆ Only post information when you wouldn't mind it showing up elsewhere—possibly without payment or credit to you.

◆ When possible, encode material with a date beyond which it won't function. While high-tech types may be able to break the code, this measure may stop plenty of others.

TIP: Put one staff member in charge of the Website. That person should keep up with new technology that might offer additional protections. Many trade associations and professional groups have committees that track how high-tech developments affect their industry.

WHAT ARE THE LEGAL PITFALLS OF SETTING PRICES?

 DRY CLEANERS ACROSS THE STREET FROM EACH other agree to close their shops the Monday after Christmas; butchers on Main Street agree to sell turkeys at a loss the week before Thanksgiving; building-supply distributors divide up a county and promise not to venture into each others' territory. All are common practices. In most places, all are illegal.

Relationships with customers and competitors are subject to federal, state, and local laws that prohibit the use of certain anticompetitive practices. Violators may face both civil and criminal penalties, including triple damages (when a penalty is figured by multiplying the damages by three) and court orders to stop the prohibited behavior. Legal actions can take the form of government enforcement cases or (more likely when a small business is involved) a private antitrust suit filed by a disgruntled customer or by a competitor.

What should you do? Or, in this case, what *shouldn't* you do? "Don't talk to your competitors unless you have to," advises James Calder, a lawyer with Rosenman & Colin in New York City. If you must talk, avoid mentioning specific business practices, such as prices, costs, discounts, and credit terms.

Involve a lawyer in any discussions of mergers or buyouts and insist on having a confidentiality agreement govern the negotiations, counsels Calder. Such a contract offers two types of protections if the deal falls through. The agreement will prohibit your competitors from using to their own advantage any confidential material you have revealed (and give you grounds for a lawsuit if they later misuse the information). It will also serve as evidence of your good-faith participation in the talks if your opponent in a subsequent lawsuit charges that they were a sham.

Check with an antitrust lawyer before making special

price deals with customers, Calder suggests. Competition is one of the primary goals of antitrust laws, so it's generally permissible to match a competitor's lower price. But certain forms of price discrimination are prohibited under a federal law known as the Robinson-Patman Act. If, for example, you charge different prices to competing customers in the same geographic area for the same goods, you may be violating the act—unless, Calder explains, you can justify the prices on the basis of cost differences or other factors.

Problems can also arise if you sell one product on the condition that the customer buy a second product—a practice known as tying. When the seller has such a substantial market share that the customer isn't free to go elsewhere, tying may be illegal. For example, the sole milk distributor for several rural counties probably would not be allowed to require his customers to buy eggs as a condition for selling them milk.

TIP: To educate your employees about this issue, Calder suggests you distribute an antitrust compliance policy. Ask workers to read it and sign a statement acknowledging that they understand its terms and will follow them. A lawyer can prepare these documents for as little as $1,000 in most cases.

FYI: State laws may prohibit other, similar anticompetitive practices. "Predatory pricing," or temporarily lowering prices below cost to drive out competition, is one example. Trade libel, or defaming a business ("Joe got the contract by bribing the purchasing manager"), is another.

Rules and Regulations

IT'S NOT JUST CORPORATE GIANTS THAT NEED TO WORRY about rules on consumer protection. Many restrictions apply even to very small shops.

WHAT OBLIGATIONS DOES THE AMERICANS WITH DISABILITIES ACT IMPOSE IN DEALING WITH CLIENTS AND CUSTOMERS?

 IF YOUR BUSINESS IS A PLACE OF "PUBLIC accommodation" (a term that includes everything from inns to shoe-repair stores) you must comply with Title III of the Americans with Disabilities Act, or ADA. This section prohibits discrimination against people with disabilities (including mental as well as physical impairments) and makes it the duty of business owners to ensure that their facilities are accessible.

Customers, clients, or the Justice Department can sue to enforce the law, and courts have wide latitude in designing remedies. In suits brought by private parties, they may order a business owner to make changes in the facility. When a case is brought by the Justice Department in response to an individual's complaint, the court may award monetary damages to the person and assess penalties against the business owner, including a fine of up to $50,000 for the first violation.

Businesses worry about these potential costs, but updating outmoded policies that may violate the law costs nothing. For instance, the Justice Department has gone after: stores that refused to admit people with Seeing Eye dogs; child-care centers that declined to care for children with a variety of disabilities; and a number of concerns that require a driver's license for identification and wouldn't accept ID cards instead. All these policies could have been corrected at no cost.

Sometimes a business needs to offer "auxiliary aids," such as amplification devices for deaf people. Title III says a company must provide such help unless it would "fundamentally alter" the nature of the goods, services, and facilities or results in an "undue burden" for the enterprise.

When "readily achievable," the law also requires removal of architectural and communication "barriers." There are no formulas for what business owners must do to comply, but good-faith efforts to improve access go a long way in protecting you from liability. If supplying a Braille menu would present an undue burden (defined as "significant difficulty or expense") for a restaurant owner, it might be enough to have a waiter read the menu to the blind customer. If it's not easy to remove stairs leading to a dry cleaner's front door, the owner may offer curbside service at no additional charge.

The most stringent requirements are those for construction of new facilities. Federal standards regulate everything from the design of checkout aisles to emergency evacuation routes. Strict rules also apply to renovating existing facilities. When altering "primary function areas," such as a bank lobby or the dining room of a restaurant, owners must provide access to people with handicaps. In addition, bathrooms, drinking fountains, and telephones must be made accessible unless the added expense is more than 20 percent of the original alteration.

TIP: There is a tax credit for eligible companies with $1 million or less in gross receipts or with 30 or fewer full-time employees that make their businesses accessible to all. The credit equals 50 percent of expenses that exceed $250 but are not more than $10,250. Claim the credit on Internal Revenue Service Form 8826—Disabled Access Credit.

FYI: For examples of good-faith efforts to make space accessible, refer to the Justice Department's *ADA Handbook* and *Highlights,* a summary of Title III rules. Both are available free from the Office on the Americans with Disabilities Act information line at 800-514-0301 (voice) or 800-514-0383 (Telecommunication Device for the Deaf).

WHAT ARE THE RULES ON MAIL-ORDER SALES?

 FEDERAL TRADE COMMISSION REGULATIONS ON mail order also apply to goods ordered by telephone, fax, and computer. The requirements are: you must usually ship merchandise by the date promised or within 30 days if you have not specified a delivery date. The clock starts running at the time you receive the order. If you can't ship on time, you must call or send a notice to let customers know about the delay, ask whether they still want the merchandise, and offer a prompt refund if they don't.

TIP: To show compliance, the FTC recommends that you keep careful records of all your communications with customers. A single violation can subject you to an FTC enforcement action, which may include a federal lawsuit and a fine of up to $10,000.

FYI: You'll find a sample notice in the FTC's free booklet, *A Business Guide to the Federal Trade Commission's Mail or Telephone Order Merchandise Rule,* available from the agency's Office of Consumer and Business Education at 202-326-3650.

HOW CAN I REDUCE THE RISK OF PRODUCT-LIABILITY LAWSUITS?

Q 82 SMALL BUSINESSES CAN BE DRAGGED INTO product-liability lawsuits when goods they manufacture, sell, lease, or service cause injury to users. Such suits stem from defects in manufacture or design or from a failure to provide adequate warning labels and instructions with the merchandise. Under rules of strict liability, sellers and manufacturers are deemed responsible for injuries resulting from these flaws and oversights. The financial consequences of a suit can be devastating, especially if you lose.

The best way to reduce exposure is to focus on the nature of the product and the circumstances surrounding its distribution. Inspect or test all articles before distributing them. Make sure that the claims in your advertising and promotional materials are truthful *(see Q75).* Monitor sales representatives to be sure they don't overstate a product's virtues; in some cases, promises about performance may be construed as warranties *(see Q83).*

Keith Gerrard, a lawyer with Perkins Coie in Seattle, advises manufacturers to consider having a written agreement (such as a sales contract or purchase order) with purchasers, disclaiming responsibility for product defects. Disclaimers won't protect manufacturers against personal-injury suits but may guard against related claims for property loss or economic damages, Gerrard says. A company also may shift responsibility through an indemnity—an agreement by some other party in the chain of distribution to defend the company or reimburse the plaintiff in case of a lawsuit.

Small businesses may not have the bargaining power to get disclaimers or indemnities from their suppliers or customers. More typically, you're the one who is asked to sign such clauses—preprinted terms in purchase orders and sales contracts that could expose you to liability.

Known as boilerplate material, these terms are less likely to stand up to legal challenge than those that have been actively negotiated. A court could find, for example, that the small firm didn't fully understand the material. But don't count on being bailed out by a court. It's a good idea to read the fine print before signing anything.

TIP: Check that all goods come with adequate instruction booklets and labels. This is a particularly important step when distributing imported products, whose instructions may be insufficient or may contain translation errors.

TIP: If you find boilerplate terms that are unacceptable, cross them out and initial each change in the margin of the contract. One possibility is that the company you're doing business with won't even notice. If it does and the objectionable clause turns out to be a deal breaker, make clear that you choose not to deal with the enterprise because of its contract. If enough other businesses do the same, the supplier or customer may eventually adopt a more lenient attitude.

AM I REQUIRED TO OFFER A WARRANTY?

NO LAW REQUIRES YOU TO OFFER A WRITTEN warranty. Whether you do or not, most state laws imply two warranties any time you sell a product to consumers. The first, the implied warranty of merchantability, applies when you sell a product that you are in business to sell. It means that the product is not defective and that it will do the things one normally expects it to do. For example, people would expect a knife to cut bread but not cement.

The second warranty, the implied warranty of fitness for a

particular purpose, applies when the seller knows the purpose for which the buyer needs the product and the buyer relies on the seller's advice. Suppose a customer tells you he needs a cleaning fluid safe for use on antique furniture and you recommend a harsh detergent. On the basis of your suggestion, he buys the product and it destroys his antique. You will have breached the warranty of fitness for a particular purpose and could be required to reimburse him for the item.

As long as you're legally bound by two implied warranties, there are good reasons to prepare your own. A written warranty shows buyers that you believe in the quality of what you're selling. Consumers consider warranties together with price and quality in deciding whether to buy a product. Offering a warranty also gives you some control over the repair, refund, or replacement of the product.

What a warranty can't do is help you avoid certain legal obligations. If you offer a written warranty, federal law usually prohibits you from disclaiming the implied ones. Nor can you generally use a warranty to avoid strict liability (*see Q82*).

If you offer a warranty for a product that costs the consumer more than $15, the Federal Trade Commission requires you to make the warranty available to the prospective purchaser. For manufacturers, this could mean attaching the warranty to the item or giving the retailer a copy of the warranty that can be displayed with the product. Retailers must display the warranty near the product or post signs in prominent locations offering consumers the warranty. Mail-order companies may print the entire warranty in the catalogue (near the warranted product or in the information section), or make a note in the catalogue (again, near the product or in the information section) indicating an address where consumers can write for a free copy of the warranty. Door-to-door sales companies must have their representatives offer to show consumers the warranty before they buy the product.

Advertising your warranty can be a powerful selling tool, but here, too, certain restrictions apply. For instance, if you advertise a warranty that offers a lifetime guarantee, the FTC requires you to specify whose lifetime you mean—the life of the product or the life of the consumer. For a money-back guarantee, FTC rules require that your advertising clearly state "any material limitations or conditions" required for the refund, such as giving back unused portions of the product or returning the item in its original packaging.

Ads should also tell customers where they can get details of the warranty. You don't need to repeat all the terms in your ad, but the FTC generally requires you to let customers know where they can look at the warranty. If your product is sold in a store, your ad must tell customers that the warranty is available there. For products sold by mail order or by telephone, the ad must tell customers how they can get free, complete details of the written warranty.

IF I OFFER A WRITTEN WARRANTY, WHAT ARE THE KEY ISSUES TO COVER?

Q 84 WARRANTIES MUST CONFORM TO BOTH STATE and federal law, so it's best to enlist a lawyer's help in drafting them. Sketching out the key elements beforehand could help save you money in legal fees. Here are some issues to consider:

◆ **Choose the type of warranty you want to extend.** Depending on the benefit you offer, your warranty will be either full or limited. Under federal law, a business can call a warranty "full" only if it meets all these requirements:

You will honor the warranty no matter who owns the product during the warranty period.

You will not charge to repair the product.

If you cannot repair the product after a reasonable number of tries, you will give the customer the choice of a replacement or a refund.

You will provide service under the warranty whether or not the consumer returns the warranty registration card.

Your warranty does not limit the length of time during which implied warranties are in effect.

For certain products, you might want to consider a "multiple" warranty—one that's full for some parts and limited for others.

◆ **Decide what service your warranty will include.** The service you provide might cover repairs, refunds, exchanges, or some combination of the three. The terms, "satisfaction guaranteed," "money-back guarantee," and "free trial offer," all suggest that you are prepared to offer a full refund. Don't use these terms unless that's what you mean.

Your warranty can include a disclaimer indicating that you will not cover damage to the product from certain uses. For example: "This warranty for the Slice and Dice food processor does not cover damage that results from alteration, accident, misuse, abuse, or neglect."

◆ **Establish a procedure for correcting the problem.** Do you want customers to send the product back to you? Take it in to the store where they bought it? Take it to an authorized service center? Will you send a repair person to their home?

◆ **Cover the essentials.** If you offer a written warranty for a product that costs the consumer more than $15, the FTC requires that the warranty provide the following information:

Who it applies to. Does it cover only the original purchaser, or will the warranty extend to subsequent owners?

What it covers. You need to be clear about what the warranty does and does not cover. For example, you may want to list specific uses of the product that are excluded from the warranty: "This warranty does not cover damage to the Squawk Box Television caused by improper connection to the equipment of other manufacturers."

What you will do if something goes wrong. Let consumers know what you will do to correct the problem. For instance, if you expect them to pay shipping costs, the warranty will need to make that clear.

When the warranty period begins and ends.

How to get service under the warranty. You should list all necessary information, including the name and address of the company and a person to contact. Alternatively, you can give a telephone number that consumers can call without charge to get further details.

How state law affects the customer's rights. You won't need to summarize the various state laws, but your warranty must include the following statement: "This warranty gives you specific legal rights, and you may also have other rights that vary from state to state."

FYI: *Writing Readable Warranties* and *A Businessperson's Guide to Federal Warranty Law* include sample warranties and are available free from the FTC's Office of Consumer and Business Education at 202-326-3650.

Contracts

HAVING A CONTRACT DOESN'T MEAN YOU AND A CUSTOMER distrust each other. In fact, by forcing you to establish rules of the game, it can help avoid disputes later.

WHEN DO I NEED A WRITTEN CONTRACT?

 OVERLY FORMAL AS IT MIGHT SOUND, A contract is a good idea in most cases, whether you're working as a consultant *(see Q86)*, renovating someone's house, or selling merchandise over the counter. In many states, the law says certain contracts aren't binding unless they're in writing. These include contracts for the sale of goods worth more than $500 and contracts that last more than one year.

For long-term relationships or other situations when conflicts could arise, a contract gives you the chance to discuss in advance how you'll resolve them *(see Q102)*. Should you wind up in court, your agreement provides evidence of the deal. Even if you never do, this document can double as a promotion tool, highlighting all you have to offer; just be sure you don't overstate your duties and wind up taking on extra work you never bargained for.

The contract between you and a customer doesn't need to be written in complex legal terms and doesn't have to be witnessed or notarized. In its simplest form, a contract involves an offer by one party, acceptance by the other, and "consideration"—a promise by each side to exchange something of value (like money for services). Faxes confirming a transaction are often all that's needed. Many businesses rely on routine purchase orders, work orders, and invoices, which can double as legal tools: they often include warranties *(see Q83–84)* and policies on returns, exchanges, or repairs, for instance. A letter of agreement, which is less intimidating than a more formal document, is just as valid legally.

Sometimes you need a more detailed agreement—for example, when your relationship involves exclusivity, a complex work schedule, your own judgment in selecting goods, approval from other parties, or a substantial sum of money. In such cases, you can keep legal costs down by summarizing the deal in your own words and getting a lawyer to "bless" it. Among the topics you may want to cover are:

◆ A description of the product you're selling or the service you're going to perform
◆ Some mention of the parties involved, including who has authority to speak for each
◆ Your return and exchange policy
◆ How and when the products or services will be delivered
◆ Payment terms
◆ Penalties for delays and circumstances that might extend a deadline without penalty
◆ Grounds for termination
◆ Restrictions on damages if the deal falls apart (so you don't wind up arguing later about who gets what)
◆ Limits on your liability
◆ Means of notifying each other (for instance, by certified mail)
◆ What state law will apply (naming your own state gives you a home-court advantage)
◆ Methods for resolving disputes *(see Chapter 7).*

Whatever form your agreement takes, it's a good idea to have a lawyer look it over. You should also enlist a lawyer's help to interpret contracts clients have drafted. When reviewing such agreements, don't be afraid to ask for changes in the provisions. However standard they may seem, most terms are negotiable.

TIP: If you deal regularly with the same kinds of products or clients, a lawyer can help you develop a form of contract that you can adapt for each client. Even when negotiations get more involved, an attorney need not be a visible player unless the customer sends legal counsel to the bargaining table or the transaction is very complex.

IF I'M WORKING AS A CONSULTANT, SHOULD I HAVE AN INDEPENDENT-CONTRACTOR AGREEMENT?

YES. HAVING A WRITTEN AGREEMENT OFFERS you a variety of legal protections. By describing work to be done, it avoids misunderstandings later. In case there's any dispute about payment, it's evidence that you were retained to do certain work. And it helps establish that you're an independent contractor, rather than an employee of the company *(see Q54)*.

It's best to involve a lawyer at the contract stage—especially if you're just starting out as a consultant or embarking on a big project. To cut legal expenses, you can verbally hash out the basics with your client beforehand. Here are some points to cover:

◆ Describe the work you're doing and when it's due.

◆ Say how you'll be paid for it (by the hour or, better yet, by the project) and when payment is due.

◆ Establish that you're performing the services as an independent contractor (not as an employee of your client) and that you have other clients.

◆ Give the starting and ending date of the work.

◆ Specify how either of you may end the agreement and how much notice you must give each other.

◆ Describe which expenses, if any, your client will reimburse.

◆ Set up a procedure for notifying each other (for instance by certified mail, to a particular person or address).

◆ Indicate which state law will govern interpretations of the agreement (naming your own state gives you a home-court advantage).

If your client prepares the first draft, be sure to have a lawyer review that, too. It may very well include terms that are unfavorable to you. Examples are: overbroad promises that you'll reimburse the client for any lawsuits arising from

SMALL BUSINESS LEGAL SMARTS

158

MARKETING PRODUCTS AND SERVICES

your work; restrictions on working for the company's competitors or other parties; penalties for work delivered late; and provisions that you sign away your intellectual property *(see Q22)* in the work.

TIP: With a contract in hand, you might be better off than employees in at least one important respect. Most staffers can lose their jobs at the boss's whim *(see Q57)*. In contrast, your clients (and you) have promises to keep before any of you may call it quits.

FYI: You can find sample forms (hard copy and a computer disk) with instructions about adapting them to your own needs in the book, *Wage Slave No More: The Independent Contractor's Legal Guide,* by Stephen Fishman (Nolo Press, $29.95).

CHAPTER 6

Getting Paid

WHEN THE SUBJECT IS
money, business owners walk a fine line. Those who
press repeatedly for payment may sour relationships
with customers. Those who adopt a more laissez-
faire approach risk never getting paid or, in effect,
giving clients an interest-free float.

Fortunately, there's another option. It starts with
establishing payment terms up front and promptly
following through on overdue accounts. Angry as
you may feel when those checks are late, try not to
take it personally—or worse yet, let it show. The
more you can treat money as one more aspect of
doing business, the greater the chances that your
diplomacy will pay off.

If it doesn't, legal action may be your only
recourse. But whether it makes financial sense is
another matter. Before you call in the lawyers or go
to small claims court, you'll want to evaluate what

the matter's worth. Your time, energy, and money might be better spent generating new business than chasing old duds.

Solid Groundwork

AT THE START OF A RELATIONSHIP, NO ONE LIKES TO think about battles over money. But should it come to that, you increase the odds of getting what's owed if you've set the rules in advance and know where to find a client's assets.

WHAT STEPS CAN I TAKE TO AVOID DEADBEAT CUSTOMERS?

 RULE NUMBER ONE IS KNOW THY CLIENT. People are most forthcoming about financial details when they open an account and are eager for your product or service. So have each new customer or client fill out a credit application or other questionnaire supplying the information you need. Ask for the individual's:

◆ Address and phone number
◆ Social Security number
◆ Driver's license number and car registration
◆ The name and branch of the customer's bank
◆ The name and address of his or her employer (if any).

Before doing business with a partnership, get these specifics on all partners, since each is fully responsible for debts and liabilities of the enterprise *(see Q1)*. If one partner doesn't pay your bill, you can collect the entire amount from the others. If a customer seems put off by your request, that might be a red flag of financial instability.

Request references from customers, scrutinize these documents, and update them annually. For clients who won't disclose the name of their banks, follow the paper trail they leave through checks given to you or cashed in the course of doing business. If you're dissatisfied with references or have doubts about the prospect of timely payment, set a short credit period or request full or partial remuneration up front.

FYI: Another way to get financial information about a customer is to purchase a credit report from one of the professional reporting agencies. When the subject of the report is a business, information comes from public records and material that the company supplies. If your customer is a small or a new company, the report may not turn up much material that you don't already have. Reports on businesses can be purchased from Dun & Bradstreet (800-765-3867) and from Experian (formerly TRW) (800-282-4879), which supplies reports only to its own subscribers.

For credit reports on individuals, federal law says you must have the person's permission first. Individual credit reports are available from Trans Union (800-916-8800) and Equifax (800-711-5341). Both these companies require that you be a subscriber. (If you're not, you can ask a company that is a member to request a report for you.)

HOW LONG SHOULD I WAIT BEFORE PRESSURING CLIENTS TO PAY?

Q 88 BEGIN YOUR COLLECTION EFFORT ON THE FIRST day the money is past due. Start with a telephone call in which you indicate that payment is late, determine whether there was any problem with your product or service, and ask when you can expect to be paid. Follow up with another call in ten days or two weeks if necessary.

When collecting from other businesses, restrict calls to the office unless the party consistently ignores your calls and messages. If contacting people at home, call during reasonable hours (not before 8 A.M. or after 9 P.M. under federal law). Don't make harassing calls (for example, by calling repeatedly or letting the phone ring incessantly).

If your telephone calls do not elicit prompt payment, send a series of three or four certified letters in which your demand for payment grows increasingly urgent. These letters, which you can later use as evidence of your collection efforts, should arrive at regular intervals over a period of several months.

Specify in the first letter the service or merchandise you haven't been paid for, the sum owed, and the date you fulfilled your obligations to the customer. Mention any phone calls in which the customer acknowledged the debt and promised to pay you. Subsequent letters can be more forceful, indicating steps that you are prepared to take, such as turning over the account to a collection agency *(see Q90)*.

TIP: If you suspect the debtor has skipped town (or might), you can mark the envelope "Address correction requested. Forwarding postage guaranteed." The post office will send you a postcard with the person or company's new address.

Always conduct yourself in a businesslike manner. Avoid insulting, sarcastic, or obscene language. Don't use deceptive tactics. These include sending documents that simulate court papers or impersonating a lawyer or debt collector. If you threaten to bring a civil lawsuit, be sure you are willing or able to carry it out. Unless you have grounds for a criminal case (it is a crime in many states to pass a bad check, for example),

Seven Deadly Debt Collection Practices

WHETHER YOU'RE A professional debt collector or just chasing your own overdue accounts, federal and state laws dictate the methods you may use. Alan D. Reffkin, a former senior trial attorney for the Federal Trade Commission and expert on collection law, offers the following list of debt collection practices that can get you into legal trouble:

1 Jeopardizing consumers' jobs by revealing the purpose of calling or writing them at work. In most states, the law permits you to contact debtors at work, but you must guard their privacy. Even when state law permits such calls, you shouldn't phone people unless company policy at the debtor's place of work allows personal calls. Never reveal to any third party that the person owes a debt.

Letters are even more risky, because of the possibility that someone else will open the mail. If you must write, mark any correspondence "personal and confidential."

2 Suggesting to any third parties (like neighbors, friends, or business associates) that a consumer is in debt. If you (or one of your employees) are calling these individuals to try and track someone down, you may only ask: Where does the debtor live? What is his or her home

don't even hint that the debtor has committed a crime.

WHAT ARE THE RULES ON IMPOSING FINANCE CHARGES?

Q 89 THIS IS A SUBJECT REGULATED BY STATE AND federal law. State law dictates how much interest you may charge. To find out what limitations apply, contact the state attorney general's office or department of consumer affairs. On the federal side, the Truth in Lending Act, which mainly protects consumers, requires you to make certain written disclosures before doing business. For an phone number? Where does he or she work? Federal law also requires you to say you are "confirming or correcting location information" about the consumer.

3 **Publicly announcing that a consumer is in debt.** This includes mentioning debts on a postcard, tacking a note on someone's door, or publishing a list of people who owe you money.

4 **Calling consumers at home during "inconvenient" times.** That generally means before 8 A.M. or after 9 P.M.

5 **Using deceptive tactics to collect information.** It's perfectly legal to encourage customers to disclose financial facts and figures. What you can't do is trick them into it. Example: sending a debtor a check, hoping he'll cash it at his bank and thereby lead you to his account.

6 **Faking documents.** This includes phony court papers and dunning letters that look like telegrams.

7 **Making empty threats. Don't say (or even imply) that you'll sue unless you intend to.** Likewise, unless you plan to notify a credit-reporting bureau about a delinquent account, avoid statements like: "nonpayment will affect your credit rating" or "delinquent accounts are often reported to credit bureaus."

"open-end" credit account (one with repeated transactions) these include:

◆ When you will start to impose a finance charge
◆ The annual interest rate
◆ The finance charge for each month or quarter (or whatever the billing cycle is)
◆ The method used to determine the balance on which the finance charge is computed
◆ A statement outlining the consumer's rights and your respon-sibilities. (The Federal Trade Commission provides a sample in Appendix G of *Regulation Z, Truth in Lending*, available

from the agency's Division of Credit Practices at 202-326-3224.) You must send it to customers at least once a year.

In addition, your periodic statements must include:

◆ A list of transactions covered

◆ The annual interest rate

◆ The finance charge for each billing cycle

◆ The balance on which the finance charge is computed

◆ The amount of any finance charge added to the account during the billing cycle

◆ The date by which the balance must be paid to avoid additional finance charges

◆ The address to be used for notice of billing errors.

Legal Recourse

WHEN DIPLOMACY DOESN'T GET RESULTS, YOU'LL WANT TO consider legal action. Unfortunately, there's a price when you stand up for your rights.

WHEN SHOULD I HIRE A COLLECTION AGENCY OR A LAWYER TO CHASE OVERDUE ACCOUNTS?

 COST IS THE CHIEF DRAWBACK OF GOING THIS route. Bill collectors typically take a third to half of accounts receivable—depending on how much money is involved, the volume of business you're offering them, and how old the debt. Even lawyers, who may charge a flat fee or bill by the hour for other kinds of matters, tend to work on contingency *(see Q39)* when handling collections.

If you have a number of accounts that require collection, you can ask a lawyer to handle the group of them for a lump sum. A young attorney eager for work might be willing to bill you by the hour. Even if your lawyer doesn't do anything you couldn't do yourself, correspondence on an attorney's letterhead could be the one thing that gets results.

Collection agencies offer another advantage: experience tracking down elusive debtors. Should you decide on this course, hire an agency that's well established in your geographical area and get several references. Ask these other businesses whether the collection agency provides monthly reports and is on time making any payments it recovers.

Before you retain the agency, request samples of the kinds of letters they send out and ask to briefly sit with their collectors to listen in on phone calls.

If you want repeat business from customers, you don't want to alienate them with a harsh collection style. If the business is closed down and you don't anticipate future dealings, you might opt for a tougher approach.

HOW EFFECTIVE IS SMALL CLAIMS COURT FOR CHASING DELINQUENT ACCOUNTS?

Q 91 WHETHER YOU'RE DEALING WITH A DELINQUENT client or with another business that failed to deliver on its promise, you may get results through small claims court. Depending on the state (and sometimes varying from one jurisdiction to another within the state), these courts handle claims of up to $1,000 to $15,000 *(see box on page 171)*. Some people will pay up as soon as you file the case. Others won't even appear in court, and you could get a judgment by default. A third possibility is that you'll win the battle and get a judgment.

Now the bad news: enforcing that judgment can be a laborious process *(see Q92)*, and there's no guarantee that you'll collect a cent. So before you go to the trouble, it pays to know whether your customer has any assets and, if so, where they are. Having current addresses lets you serve people with court papers and avoid the need to hire a private investigator to help find someone. The best time to get this information is before the relationship turns sour *(see Q87)*.

To be sure that your judgment is enforceable, it's important to sue the right person in the right court. Sue individual customers in the county in which they live. Sue corporate clients in the county in which their company does business. If the company owners are personally responsible *(see Q1)*, you also can sue in the county in which they live.

Whether the owners are personally responsible will depend largely on the business format of the company you're suing. With a sole proprietorship, you can sue the person both individually and as the business owner. When suing a partnership the same principle applies, since each partner is fully responsible for all debts and liabilities of the partnership *(see Q1)*. A judgment against a corporation or a limited liability company gives you the right to recover only against the business *(see Q1)*, to the extent that it has any assets.

Your goal in court will be to show you were not paid for a service you performed or a product you delivered. Bring purchase orders, invoices, or correspondence confirming the transaction, and for tangible items, proof of delivery and a sample or photo of the item sold.

Follow-up letters you sent the customer *(see Q88)* can show your efforts to negotiate payment schedules or accommodate any customer complaints. This correspondence, along with any letters from the customer acknowledging the debt, might also prove that your demands for payment have been unfruitful. Just in case you need testimony from witnesses, determine who among your employees was involved in the sale or collection efforts.

TIP: Once you have a gripe, don't postpone suing. You may have trouble catching up with the customer or the statute of limitations (five to seven years in most places) may expire, preventing you from bringing a case.

FYI: *Everybody's Guide to Small Claims Court,* by Ralph Warner (Nolo Press, $18.95), leads readers through the small claims process—from evaluating whether you have a case, to collecting a judgment.

HOW DO I COLLECT A SMALL CLAIMS COURT JUDGMENT?

 PROCEDURES VARY BY STATE AND WITHIN EACH state are defined by local court clerks and sheriffs' offices. Ask the clerks in these offices about the exact steps to take. Meanwhile, here are some general guidelines to increase your odds of collecting:

◆ **Demand payment.** Send your opponent (known as the judgment debtor) a certified letter with a copy of the

Small Claims Limits

THE MAXIMUM DOLLAR amount you can sue for in
Small Claims courts varies from state to state:

ALABAMA	$ 3,000		NEVADA	3,500
ALASKA	5,000		NEW HAMPSHIRE	2,500
ARIZONA	2,500		NEW JERSEY	2,000
ARKANSAS	3,000		NEW MEXICO	5,000
CALIFORNIA	5,000		NORTH DAKOTA	5,000
COLORADO	5,000		OHIO	3,000
CONNECTICUT	2,000		OKLAHOMA	4,500
DELAWARE*	15,000		OREGON	2,500
DISTRICT OF COLUMBIA	5,000		PENNSYLVANIA	10,000
FLORIDA	5,000		RHODE ISLAND	1,500
GEORGIA	5,000		SOUTH CAROLINA	10,000
HAWAII	3,500		SOUTH DAKOTA	4,000
IDAHO	3,000		TENNESSEE	10,000
ILLINOIS	2,500		TEXAS	5,000
INDIANA	3,000		UTAH	5,000
KENTUCKY	1,500		VERMONT	3,500
LOUISIANA	2,000		VIRGINIA	1,000
MAINE	3,000		WASHINGTON	2,500
MARYLAND	1,000		WEST VIRGINIA	10,000
MASSACHUSETTS	2,000		IOWA	4,000
MICHIGAN	1,750		KANSAS	1,800
MINNESOTA	5,000		NEW YORK	3,000
MISSISSIPPI	1,000		NORTH CAROLINA	3,000
MISSOURI	3,000		WISCONSIN	5,000
MONTANA	3,000		WYOMING	2,000
NEBRASKA	2,100			

*CALLED "JUSTICE OF THE PEACE" COURTS

judgment enclosed. In the letter, reiterate your claim, point
out the need to honor the judgment, and demand payment
by return mail. You may want to negotiate a payment
schedule.

TIP: Act quickly to enforce your judgment. That means within two weeks of getting the judgment, or in states that permit appeals (the period to appeal is usually between 10 and 30 days), within two weeks of the time that right expires.

◆ **Locate assets.** Some states require the person or business to provide you with a list of assets. In others, you must ask for it.

The name for the procedure varies from state to state—"interrogatory," "deposition," "citation to discover assets," "order of examination of assets," and "judgment debtor's examination" are some of the common terms. Get the appropriate form from the clerk of the court. Take the form to the sheriff, who will serve it on the debtor.

You can ask for information about many kinds of assets, including car title, bank account numbers, boats, personal property, stocks and bonds. For individuals, certain kinds of assets are protected from judgment creditors. Depending on the state, these may include retirement accounts, cash-value life insurance policies, and at least a portion of the equity in a home.

Another thing to ask about is third parties who owe money to the debtor. You can require that this money be paid directly to you to satisfy the judgment. Some states also permit you to ask whether the judgment debtor is carrying cash and to seize it at the hearing.

◆ **Seize the assets.** This process goes by a number of names, including "attachment," "garnishment," or "levying against the property." To have assets seized, you must get what is usually called a "writ of execution" or a "writ of garnishment"—a court's permission for you to ask the sheriff or marshal to seize property. Most often, you apply for this writ in the office of the small claims clerk and then take the writ to the sheriff or marshal.

Here are some of the types of property you can attach:

Bank accounts. Garnishment of a bank account may be the quickest way to get cash, provided there's money in the account. If you're suing a business, you should take your paperwork to the sheriff with instructions to show up the day before payday, a time when there is likely to be enough money in the account to satisfy your judgment.

Business assets. In some states you can levy against company property such as furniture and equipment. If the enterprise operates mostly on cash, you also can garnish the money in the cash register. Again, pick a time when the register is likely to be full.

Wages. To satisfy claims against employed people, garnish their wages. This means the employer subtracts a certain amount from each paycheck until your claim is paid. State law may impose restrictions that make wage garnishment a slow way of getting paid.

Personal property. Some states have limits on seizure of personal property, exempting items like clothing and furniture. If you seize someone's car, the sheriff can require that the car be sold and that you be paid from the proceeds of the sale.

Real property. In some states, getting a judgment against a person automatically puts a lien against his or her land, meaning that you must be paid before the property can be sold or the mortgage can be refinanced. Elsewhere, you have to take the judgment to the county property recorder's office in the county in which the real estate is located in order to create a lien.

◆ **Follow up on the judgment.** Even if your initial attempts to collect prove fruitless, stay current about the judgment debtor's whereabouts and assets. Most judgments last at least seven years and can be renewed. Keep track of the renewal date so you don't lose that chance to make your claim pay off.

FYI: *Collect Your Court Judgment,* by Gini Graham Scott, Stephen R. Elias, and Lisa S. Goldoftas (Nolo Press, $19.95), is devoted entirely to enforcing a judgment. Legal rules in this book apply just to California, but the volume is full of practical information that people in other states can use.

WHAT CAN I DO WHEN A CUSTOMER GOES BANKRUPT?

WHEN A CUSTOMER FILES FOR BANKRUPTCY, chances are a creditor will collect only a small fraction of what he or she is owed, says David Gray Carl-

State Rules

RULES FOR COLLECTING a small claims judgment vary from state to state. Here are 10 questions to ask about key rules in the state where you are suing:

◆ What is the maximum amount you can sue for in small claims court?

◆ Is there a right to appeal a judgment, and if so, how long does that right apply?

◆ Are there exemptions or other restrictions that apply to garnishment of wages or bank accounts?

◆ What personal property is exempt from garnishment?

◆ What are the rules about garnishing it to vehicles?

◆ Does the state have a homestead exemption (preventing at least some of a person's equity in their home from being used to satisfy a judgment)?

◆ How long are judgments valid, and may they be renewed?

◆ If the judgment may be renewed, when must I apply for the renewal?

◆ What is the prejudgment interest rate (interest on the debt from the time it's due until the date of the judgment)?

◆ What fees are assigned to the various steps in the collection process?

son, a professor at the Benjamin N. Cardozo School of Law at Yeshiva University in New York City. That's because the law is designed to relieve debtors of obligations they can't pay.

The two most widely used alternatives for firms that need this help are Chapter 7 of the bankruptcy law, under which a firm's assets are sold to pay creditors, and Chapter 11, which permits an outfit to continue doing business while paying its debts under court supervision.

If a customer has taken advantage of either of these bankruptcy provisions, you must file a "proof-of-claim form" with the bankruptcy court in order to be eligible for payment. As a creditor, you also should submit any documents such as receipts or contracts that show what you're owed. If the debtor has listed you among its creditors in its court filing, the court will send you a proof-of-claim form. If you don't receive one, call a bankruptcy court (listed in the U.S. government pages of the phone book).

For a Chapter 7 proceeding, you must file a proof-of-claim form within 90 days of the first date set by the court for a meeting of the company's creditors. During that gathering, a trustee will be ratified; the creditors may choose their own trustee, but usually one is appointed by the U.S. Trustee's Office. Officials of the debtor firm are required by law to be present and to answer all creditors' questions under oath. Attending may provide you with valuable information about the company's assets and your prospects of recovering what you're owed.

After that, it's up to the trustee to locate the debtor's assets and distribute them. Secured creditors, such as lenders holding mortgages, are guaranteed the value of their collateral. If there is any additional property, the debtor's lawyers and accountants are paid next. Trade creditors, such as suppliers, share whatever's left. When the money runs out, most remaining debts are "discharged," or legally forgiven.

For a reorganization under Chapter 11, the deadline for filing the proof of claim is set by the court. The debtor company, which remains in business while restructuring its operations, may offer to renegotiate the terms of its debt to you—perhaps by stretching out payments over a long period. Should you fail to renegotiate, the court may eventually impose a settlement. If you receive such an offer, consult an attorney.

TIP: Act quickly; deadlines for filing the proof-of-claim form are strictly enforced, and you must meet them in order to recover anything.

FYI: If you can't collect a debt and have already reported the money due as income, you may be able to claim a bad debt deduction on your federal income tax return *(see Q114)*.

CHAPTER 7

Resolving Disputes

ONFLICTS ARE A FACT OF BUSINESS LIFE, but they don't have to destroy your company or bust your legal budget. Increasingly, small companies are handling the usual business disputes—with suppliers, customers, and employees—through mediation and other methods of alternative dispute resolution (or ADR). These companies typically agree, either before or after a lawsuit has been filed, to attempt an out-of-court resolution with the help of an impartial third party such as a lawyer, retired judge, or company that offers ADR services *(see Q104)*.

Some ADR procedures, such as binding arbitration *(see Q97)* and private judging *(see Q99)*, are basically a quick form of litigation, in that they involve a third-party decision maker with authority to impose a resolution if the parties so desire. Other procedures, such as mediation *(see Q97)* and the minitrial *(see Q98)*, are collaborative: an impartial mediator helps a group of individuals or entities with divergent views reach a goal or complete a task to their mutual satisfaction. Arbitration, mediation, and the minitrial tend to be the mechanisms most often used and, for many people, are synonymous with the term "ADR."

To prevent business problems from escalating into legal ones, it's an even better idea to anticipate conflicts before they arise. You can do that by including dispute resolution clauses in business contracts. Some simply state that in case of disagreement, both parties will try negotiation, followed by mediation, before they resort to litigation.

Conflict Resolution Methods

ADR INCLUDES A RANGE OF PRACTICES FOR QUICKLY resolving disputes at modest cost and with minimal damage to ongoing relationships. These processes, marked by confidentiality if you choose, significantly broaden dispute resolution options beyond litigation.

WHAT ARE THE PROS AND CONS OF ALTERNATIVE DISPUTE RESOLUTION?

Q 94 ADR HAS GROWN INCREASINGLY POPULAR, primarily because it is faster and cheaper than litigation. Unlike a lawsuit, which can drag on for years, ADR may resolve differences in a matter of months or even days. In the process, disputes remain confidential because ADR proceedings generally aren't a matter of public record.

Exact savings are hard to quantify, but ADR has the potential to trim tens or hundreds of thousands of dollars from a company's legal expenses. A fast resolution generally reduces lawyers' fees. ADR's streamlined procedures may also lower or eliminate the expense of "discovery"—the stage before a trial in which each side defines the issues at stake and learns the strengths and weaknesses of its case.

With ADR you have a much better shot at preserving supplier and customer relationships because the methods emphasize a cooperative, rather than adversarial, approach. That means business owners can devise solutions that might not be available in court. In a dispute over a purchase contract, for example, you might supplement a monetary settlement with an agreement to do a certain amount of business together in the future.

ADR can be especially useful in cases where the nature of your liability is unclear and potential damages are high. Examples are: disputes over intellectual property, personal injury, and employment issues. ADR can even be used to settle your differences with codefendants in a complex lawsuit. In construction cases, for example, the codefendants may spend years in court trying to shift the blame to each other. With ADR, you can cooperate in a joint defense and then negotiate, mediate, or arbitrate with your codefendants. This keeps the proceedings from dragging on.

These techniques also work well in disputes with other

small companies, the government, or customers. With claims of $100,000 or less, in fact, the cost of litigating may quickly exceed the amount at stake. Whether you're the plaintiff or the defendant, a speedy resolution can prevent too much damage to the bottom line.

Of course, ADR is not always the best route. If you're not worried about jeopardizing a business relationship and the claim is very small, you might be better off in small claims court *(see Q91)*. ADR tends to leave many stones unturned, and it may be hard to evaluate the reasonableness of a proposed settlement without full discovery.

When using ADR, you generally cannot take advantage of the so-called "provisional remedies," which allow participants in a lawsuit to ensure that assets are available to pay a future judgment. While a court could seize a piece of property or attach a paycheck, third-party neutrals cannot take such measures without authorization from the parties involved.

And unlike a court, where the judge's services are free, with ADR you have to pay the neutral third party who helps resolve a case. That can cost anywhere from several hundreds to several thousands of dollars a day, a fee that's generally split between both parties in the dispute. Of course, you won't mind paying this fee if ADR gets the case resolved without a trial. But if it doesn't, you've conceivably added many additional thousands to your legal bill.

HOW CAN I DECIDE WHETHER TO SETTLE OR SUE?

 CONSIDER THE STRENGTHS AND WEAKNESSES OF your position, the possibility of winning, and how long it might take to litigate such a case. ADR is generally better when the likelihood of winning or losing is unclear and when the attorneys' fees for litigation may vastly exceed the cost of settling. Especially when small sums are in issue, the wear and tear of a courtroom battle may not be worth the cost—even if you feel confident that you're right on the merits.

Litigation can be a better choice when you want to deter similar lawsuits or set industry precedent. If an employee you fire files a discrimination suit, for example, you may

Settle or Sue?

THE CHOICE OF whether to settle or sue will depend on your goals, your finances, and your relationship with the other side. Here are 10 questions to ask:

QUESTION	SETTLE	SUE
Do you want to continue doing business together?	YES	NO
Can your opponent afford higher legal bills?	YES	NO
Do you want to set a precedent?	NO	YES
Do you care about having some say in the outcome of the case?	YES	NO
Is it a goal to discourage similar conflicts in the future?	NO	YES
Do you care about resolving the case as quickly as possible?	YES	NO
Do you want to avoid publicity?	YES	NO
Do you want a court to decide who's right and who's wrong?	NO	YES
Does the case involve issues besides money?	YES	NO
Do you trust the other side to negotiate in good faith?	YES	NO

decide to spend time and money on litigation to prevent similar claims. In doing so, you send a message to future litigants that you plan to fight workplace cases. You may even invest more in the matter than you think it's worth to show that you're not going to roll over and settle.

In the end, more than 90 percent of all lawsuits wind up settling. Whether you'll be able to resolve a conflict before filing a case or must do so on the courthouse steps will depend on your goals, your finances, and your relationship with the other side. By settling, you give up the chance to have clear winners and losers (and perhaps a shot at the jackpot). Some people can't resist the prospect of a day in court.

At the heart of most successful dispute resolution efforts is a willingness by both sides to compromise. You and your adversary may not start out equally enthusiastic about the idea—maybe because one party can afford higher legal bills or wants to hurt the other with the negative publicity of a suit. But eventually you must get to the bargaining table. That's more likely to happen when the case involves issues besides money (giving you the chance to come up with a creative solution), you have a relationship that you want to preserve, and you're both willing to negotiate in good faith.

One of the most important decisions is whether to accept a substantial settlement offer. People gambling on a bigger win (and the publicity that goes with it) might be tempted to turn the offer down. But keep in mind that you might not do as well in court. Lawyers call this the "litigation risk"—the chance that you'll lose a case or get a smaller award and wind up with a fistful of legal bills.

HOW CAN I BECOME A BETTER NEGOTIATOR?

 NEGOTIATION IS ONE OF THE MOST IMPORTANT tools in most forms of conflict resolution. One of my favorite books on the subject is the 1981 classic *Getting to Yes: Negotiating Agreement Without Giving In*, by Roger Fisher and William Ury (Penguin Books, $11.95). Long before the phrase "win-win solution" became popular, these authors were urging negotiators to come up with options that satisfy everyone.

Fisher and Ury focus on understanding the other side and finding common ground. Their core negotiating techniques are "separating the people from the problem" and distinguishing "positions" (the concrete terms and conditions that the parties demand) from "interests" (peoples' underlying motivations, needs, desires, fears, and aspirations).

When the negotiator has tried everything else, it may be time to suspend diplomacy and play hardball. To win in the power game, these authors suggest identifying your "best alternative to a negotiated agreement" (or BATNA), whether it's walking away from the deal or going to court. The tricky part is presenting that alternative to the other side as a warning, rather than as a threat.

The Fisher-Ury method isn't perfect. If money is the only issue, probing for interests might not work—even when an

Brainstorming Basics

SOME PEOPLE THINK the term "brainstorming" just means having a single bright idea. As a conflict resolution tool, however, brainstorming goes much further. It's a way to prepare for negotiation, expand what you offer at the bargaining table, and even break a deadlock with the other side. Andrea Kupfer Schneider, a professor at Marquette University Law School, in Milwaukee, and coauthor of the book *Beyond Machiavelli: Tools for Coping with Conflict* (Harvard University Press, $16.95), suggests these tips for running a brainstorming session:

◆ Schedule a special occasion and identify the time as a session to be devoted uniquely to coming up with new ideas.

◆ Make it clear that the group will not agree upon any proposals or make any decisions at this meeting.

◆ Create an environment that is substantially different from that of routine meetings. For example, you can hold the session at an unusual time (evening, all day, a weekend), at an unusual place (country house, outdoors, social club), or under unusual conditions (participants sit in a circle or side-by-side facing a moderator).

◆ Consider breaking a large group into smaller working groups that can tackle different aspects of the problem.

◆ Announce a rule against negative comments. This rule should be strictly enforced, especially during the early part of a session.

◆ Encourage the group to develop many new and different ideas without attributing them to any single participant.

◆ Assign a "facilitator" to lead the session and record every idea on a board or flip chart visible to everyone. These roles can be filled by one person, but it is easier with two. (They can step out of role temporarily to contribute their own ideas to the list.)

◆ Plan a separate session for evaluating and criticizing ideas and then selecting the most promising ones for follow-up discussions.

impartial observer steps in to mediate. A second edition of the book (published in 1991, with Bruce Patton as a third co-author) includes a section responding to questions about the original text. Some of the toughest queries—"What do I do if people are the problem?" and "Can the way I negotiate really make a difference if the other side is more powerful?"—aren't easy to answer.

Still, the Fisher-Ury methods succeed in many settings. Next time you lock horns with a customer or vendor in what seems like a no-win situation, try using the *Getting To Yes* method. Make a list of both sets of interests and positions. Figure out ways to meet the other side's needs without selling out your own. And decide on your BATNA.

Whatever the outcome, taking these steps will greatly strengthen your negotiating hand. You still may not get exactly what you want. But at least you'll play a role in the final result.

WHAT IS THE DIFFERENCE BETWEEN ARBITRATION AND MEDIATION?

Q 97 MEDIATION IS AN INFORMAL AND VOLUNTARY dispute resolution method in which you and your adversary meet to negotiate a settlement that suits both sides. One benefit is that you won't have a decision imposed on you by a judge or arbitrator. That makes mediation useful in cases involving an ongoing relationship, when an imposed decision could plant the seeds for future discord.

Rather than have lawyers battle it out, each company sends a management representative with the authority to settle. The executive should be familiar with the dispute, but mediation sometimes works best if the person has not been directly involved in the conflict and has less personal stake in the outcome. That way, he or she will be more open to a possible compromise.

During the proceedings, an impartial third party, known as the "mediator" *(see Q104)*, meets with each side and conducts joint sessions to help you reach an agreement. The mediator's role can take various forms. Mediators who favor a "facilitative" style encourage parties to generate their own options and will not suggest settlement terms. At the other end of the spectrum are "evaluative" mediators, who will make proposals and urge parties to compromise. An evaluative mediator might assess the merits of claims or defenses, liability or damages, or predict the likely outcome of the case in court. Generally, mediators need background or expertise in the relevant area of law to make such assessments.

FYI: *How to Mediate Your Dispute,* by Peter Lovenheim (Nolo Press, $18.95), is a thorough guide to the subject, written by a mediator. It includes a brief section on arbitration and an extensive chapter on handling a mediation if you decide to represent yourself *(see Q103).*

Mediation Procedure for Business Disputes covers ground rules for the proceeding, including choosing the mediator, presenting the case, and finalizing settlement terms. It is available for $8 on a disk (which also includes a model minitrial procedure, rules for arbitration, and sample ADR contract clauses) from the CPR Institute for Dispute Resolution (formerly the Center for Public Resources), a New York nonprofit that promotes the use of ADR (212-949-6490). The material is free on the group's Website (http://www.cpradr.org).

Unlike mediation, which allows you to reach your own settlement, in arbitration you bring your case before an arbitrator or a panel of three arbitrators, whose decision is final and binding. In choosing to arbitrate, you give up your right to sue and, in most cases, any prospect of appealing the decision. Only in rare cases, when a court finds abuse of an arbitrator's discretion, can you get the award overturned.

Arbitration may be less costly and adversarial than litigation, but many experts consider it a last resort—to be used only if negotiation and mediation fail. The primary reason: arbitrators can grant any remedy or relief they believe is just and equitable, and companies often complain that they "split the baby" by simply requiring painful concessions from both sides. In addition, the chances that both parties are going to be happy with the result are greater if they reach a resolution themselves, rather than entrust their fate to a third party.

On the other hand, arbitration can eliminate years spent in the appellate process because the arbitrator's decision usually cannot be appealed. Disputes that are essentially factual (as opposed to those that involve application of legal principles) can be resolved quickly by an arbitrator, especially if he or she has expertise in your industry.

TIP: Arbitration can generate many of the expenses of a traditional lawsuit: parties to the dispute often take sworn testimony and collect evidence, increasing both clerical costs and attorneys' fees.

TIP: If you decide to arbitrate a dispute, ask the arbitrator to issue a written decision explaining the basis for the award.

WHAT IS A MINITRIAL?

THIS FORM OF ADR IS MORE FORMAL AND COSTLY than mediation because it usually includes a discovery period *(see Q94)* and a highly choreographed proceeding. Even so, the minitrial operates in a shorter time frame than a full-blown lawsuit; it's possible to settle a case within 90 days.

The centerpiece of a minitrial is an "information exchange," in which a manager or lawyer *(see Q103)* from each side presents a summary of its case before a panel of managers—typically just one from each party—and an impartial third person (a "neutral") *(see Q104)* who leads the proceedings. The panel members then meet to confidentially negotiate the settlement (so you may want to sit on the panel and let one of your managers present the case). In preparation, you and your adversary may agree to a modified form of discovery and exchange exhibits, briefs, and other documents. These are submitted to the neutral as well.

The theory behind the information exchange is that each party will gain a better understanding of the other's position *(see Q96)*. This, in turn, should lead to a more realistic stance in the negotiations to follow, a process that could take hours or extend for many weeks. When requested by the par-

Getting to the Table

COLLABORATIVE ADR PROCESSES, like mediation or a minitrial, will never succeed if your adversaries won't even come to the bargaining table. Here are some arguments that may convince them to try ADR:

◆ Disputes remain confidential because the proceedings aren't a matter of public record.

◆ There's no risk: either party may withdraw at any time, and if you don't reach a settlement, you can still go to court.

◆ You can reach a resolution together, instead of having one imposed on you by a court. That could lead to creative solutions that wouldn't be available in litigation.

◆ You would like to do business again together in the future (assuming that's true).

◆ You can both save money and resolve the case more quickly than you could in court.

◆ Before starting, you will agree on the ground rules. They may include limited discovery (see Q94), if necessary.

◆ If you can't agree to resolve all the issues through ADR, maybe you could address at least some of them that way. (If you succeed with these, it may provide a natural transition to eventually handling the entire case through ADR.)

◆ To lead the proceedings, you will choose a neutral third party who is acceptable to you both. (Although the parties typically share the cost of this professional, you can offer to pay for an initial meeting to get an objective opinion about whether ADR would be fruitful.)

ties, however, the neutral may mediate and propose settlement terms (see Q97). If settlement efforts fail, you're free to go ahead with a trial.

The minitrial's goal of ferreting out information makes it particularly well suited to complex cases arising from high-stakes deals such as a joint venture, partnership, or major construction project. Minitrials have also helped resolve wrongful termination, antitrust, and product liability disputes.

With managers playing an active role in the process, the outcome tends to be more creative and business-oriented than the win-lose approach of arbitration or litigation. But as in mediation, you're paying an independent third party to help resolve the case *(see Q94)*. Depending on how many hours of his or her time you ring up, the cost could be substantial—particularly if the minitrial doesn't settle the case and you wind up going to court.

In proposing a minitrial to the other side *(see box at left)*, you can emphasize the flexibility of the proceeding, the advantages of ADR generally *(see Q94)*, and the option of litigating the dispute if your settlement efforts don't pan out. The process begins with a written agreement in which both sides designate the people who will represent their companies at the information exchange. A sample agreement, along with a timetable and other guidelines for conducting the minitrial, are available from the CPR Institute for Dispute Resolution (212-949-6490). The material is free on the group's Website (http://www.cpradr.org) or can be purchased on a disk for $8. (The disk also includes a model mediation procedure.)

WHAT IS PRIVATE JUDGING?

Q 99 THIS GENERAL TERM DESCRIBES VARIOUS situations in which adversaries retain a neutral— often a retired judge—to hear and decide their case. Sometimes the parties undertake private judging by mutual agreement before a case has been filed. More often, there's a lawsuit in progress, but state law allows the parties to hire their own judge instead of waiting for a day in court.

Such arrangements are sometimes referred to by the colloquial term "rent-a-judge." Usually the disputants have a choice about who decides the case and more flexibility in customizing dispute resolution procedures than they have in a public proceeding. Although the judge's decision tends to be binding, it can usually be appealed.

Rules on private judging vary from state to state. Typically this process is a way around publicity and generating a public record. How much the public court is involved (whether it must approve the neutral and whether that individual's decision takes the place of a public judge's) may also depend on the arrangement.

Critics of private judging argue that it is unfair, since it creates a two-tiered system of justice in which people who can afford to rent a judge get speedier (and perhaps superior) results. Another objection is to the "brain drain" that results when judges prematurely retire from the bench to pursue this more lucrative option. Still, for a company that wants to avoid crowded court dockets and get back to business, private judging may be an efficient—and economical—option.

FYI: JAMS/Endispute, a nationwide company based in Irvine, Calif., pioneered the use of private judging and is one of the many ADR providers *(see Q104)* that offers such services. Call 800-352-5267 to reach the office nearest you.

WHAT IS THE DIFFERENCE BETWEEN ADMINISTERED AND NONADMINISTERED ADR?

Q 100 THIS IS A DISTINCTION YOU SHOULD KNOW about when selecting a company that provides ADR services *(see Q104)*, known as an "ADR provider." "Administered" ADR generally means that there's some business or organization actively managing the case. Its services, charged to the adversaries, may include matching the two sides with a mediator or arbitrator, finding (or supplying) a place for them to meet, distributing documents, and scheduling sessions.

The alternative is nonadministered ADR, managed solely by the parties. Here opponents, presumably with the help of their lawyers *(see Q103)*, find an impartial third party, develop an ADR procedure, and initiate the process on their own. This option tends to avoid bureaucracy, reduce costs, and be more efficient than relying on an intermediary.

Sometimes opponents who prefer nonadministered ADR want the assistance of some third party in getting to the bargaining table and choosing the person who will help resolve the dispute. In that case, they may call in an ADR provider *(see Q104)* to supply these limited services.

HOW CAN I STOP SMALL CONFLICTS FROM ESCALATING INTO LARGER ONES?

 BY PRACTICING PREVENTIVE LAW, YOU CAN squelch budding problems before they become full-fledged disputes. Here are three ways to do that:

1 **Partnering.** Typically used for large construction projects, this dispute prevention method can be replicated in other settings, particularly in joint ventures. Before the work starts, parties to the project generally assemble for a several-day retreat away from their organizations. With the help of an impartial third party, they get to know each other, discuss some of the likely rough spots in the project, and even settle on a process to resolve misunderstandings and disputes as the project progresses.

2 **Step negotiation.** With this dispute resolution method, the two people who are most intimately involved in a conflict first try to solve it at their level. If they fail, their immediate supervisors, who are not as closely entangled in the issue, are asked to confer and attempt a resolution. If they also fail, the problem is passed on to the next higher management level in both companies, with authority to settle. This process may require too many levels to be used in a tiny company, but it could work well in other small businesses that have clearly defined departments and lines of authority.

Step negotiation can be especially useful in business relationships that spawn frequent disagreements, such as those involving a joint venture. In this case, the negotiation process forces everyone to keep talking. It also gives managers at both companies an incentive to resolve a problem before it reaches their boss's desk.

3 **A "deadlock" clause.** With certain types of business arrangements, such as a partnership in which both sides have equal weight, a "deadlock" clause can be used to designate a third party who will cast the deciding vote when a conflict arises. In these situations, a stalemate could hold up a critical decision, such as whether to acquire another firm.

However, when applied to day-to-day management issues, such as hiring decisions or competitive strategies, a deadlock clause could have a polarizing effect. Knowing they always have a tiebreaker, the parties don't get in the habit of compromising. Instead, they routinely live with decisions made by someone outside the company. A better choice, if principals can't resolve management issues themselves, is to call a mediator who can help forge a consensus.

WHAT IS THE BEST WAY TO INITIATE ADR?

Q 102 WHEN EMOTIONS FLARE OVER A DISPUTE already in progress, you may need a neutral just to get negotiations rolling. Here are two ways to sidestep this problem:

1 **Include ADR clauses in business agreements.** In the most scaled down version, these "predispute" clauses simply state that in case of a conflict, both parties will attempt a resolution through ADR before they resort to litigation. They also specify which ADR method will be used. More complex variations of the clause name the neutral agency to handle the case and the rules that will apply.

Predispute agreements requiring arbitration of consumer disputes or entered into as a condition of employment *(see Q59)* have generated substantial backlash lately from people who argue that these take-it-or-leave-it contracts are unfair and against public policy. A more effective approach is to engage in a progressive series of dispute resolution procedures. One step typically is some form of negotiation, preferably face-to-face between the parties. If that's unsuccessful, the next step may be mediation or another facilitated settlement effort. If no resolution has been reached at any of the earlier stages, the agreement can provide for binding resolution through arbitration.

Depending on whether you prefer to start with nonbinding procedures or go right to a binding one, here are some sample clauses:

Negotiation, with Mediation or Minitrial if Necessary
If a dispute arises out of this contract, the parties will try to resolve it promptly by negotiation between executives. If the dispute has not been resolved by negotiation within [30]

days, the parties will try to settle the dispute through medi-
ation [minitrial].

If these nonbinding procedures are unsuccessful, you're presumably free to go to court.

Negotiation, Followed by Mediation, with Arbitration if Necessary

If a dispute arises out of this contract, the parties will try to resolve it promptly by negotiation between executives. If the dispute has not been resolved by negotiation within [30] days, the parties will try to settle the dispute through mediation. Any controversy that remains unresolved [30] days after appointment of a mediator will go to arbitration. The place of arbitration will be [_____]. Unless the parties agree otherwise, any award will be in writing and state the reasons for the award. Judgment upon the award may be entered by any court having jurisdiction of the case.

This clause calls for you to try nonbinding procedures (negotiation, followed by mediation), and move on to a binding one (arbitration) if that's unsuccessful. If you go that final step, however, you and your customers give up the right to sue over the matter at issue.

Arbitration Clause

If a dispute arises out of this contract, the parties will resolve it by arbitration. The place of arbitration will be [_____]. Unless the parties agree otherwise, any award will be in writing and state the reasons for the award. Judgment on the award may be entered by any court having jurisdiction of the case.

By agreeing to this clause, you and your customers would generally be bound by the decision of the arbitrator and could not appeal that ruling in court. Many contracts refer to the rules that will govern the arbitration. Typically, they are the rules of the American Arbitration Association (212-484-4000), which contemplate administered arbitration *(see Q100).* Another option is the rules of the CPR Institute for

Dispute Resolution (212-949-6490), which refer to non-administered arbitration.

2 **Invoke an ADR pledge.** At the urging of the CPR Institute, more than 800 of the nation's largest companies have signed a corporate policy statement agreeing to attempt ADR with other companies that have made the same pledge. Approximately 1,500 law firms have signed a similar pledge, promising to discuss ADR with clients "where appropriate."

These statements aren't as strong as contract clauses, but they can provide a useful tool for persuading other businesses (and their lawyers) to use ADR. When a dispute arises, you can check to see whether the other company (or its law firm) has signed the policy statement. If so, it can help you initiate ADR without implying any lack of confidence in your case.

FYI: To find out whether a particular company or law firm has signed the CPR Institute statement, contact the group at 212-949-6490, or check its Website at http://www.cpradr.org.

ADR Practicalities

THESE DAYS ANYONE CAN HANG OUT A SHINGLE AND CALL themselves a specialist in conflict resolution. There are no specific licensing standards in the field, so you may find a wide range of experience, abilities, and quality. You'll want to carefully check credentials before enlisting their help.

DO I NEED A LAWYER TO REPRESENT ME IN ADR?

Q 103 WITH BINDING ADR PROCESSES, SUCH AS arbitration and private judging, you'll want a lawyer to represent you, just as if you were going to court. In nonbinding procedures, such as mediation and the minitrial, your lawyer can take a more backseat role; many cases get resolved by business executives without their lawyers being present.

That said, even with nonbinding ADR, it's a good idea to have a lawyer involved—at least behind the scenes—throughout the process. In the early stages, a lawyer can offer an opinion about the issues at stake, advise you about what type of dispute resolution method might be most effective, and help draw up some ground rules for the proceedings. If a lawsuit has already been filed, you may want a lawyer's help to keep courtroom activity at bay while you pursue ADR.

Whether you negotiate alone will depend on how complex the issues are, how much money is at stake, and how comfortable you feel bargaining for yourself. You may decide to have a lawyer do all the talking; listen quietly, prepared to step in as needed; or just be available by telephone for any questions that come up.

Either way, you'll want to put something in writing as soon as you reach an agreement. Most likely this will be just a draft that you take with you when you leave the session. Even if your lawyer wasn't present, you'll want his or her help preparing the final settlement agreement.

FYI: The *Martindale-Hubbell Dispute Resolution Directory,* available in some libraries, is a giant reference book listing more than 60,000 professionals involved in dispute resolution. It includes judges, attorneys, law firms, and other experts, with information on practice areas and services provided.

HOW SHOULD I CHOOSE AN ADR PROVIDER?

Q 104 WITH THE GROWING POPULARITY OF ADR, many private companies and nonprofit groups now offer neutrals for hire.

Third-party neutrals may be nonlawyers, practicing lawyers, or retired judges. While the neutral needn't have a law degree, in some cases it may be helpful or even necessary. Lawyers are sensitive to the possibility that negotiations will fail, so they may set up a streamlined method of exchanging information without prejudicing either side if the parties decide to go to court.

Using a judge as your neutral has its pros and cons. A judge has the parliamentary skills to run a meeting and credibility because he or she has heard so many cases. But a judge may inject a formality into the proceeding that makes it reminiscent of the courtroom and destroys the mood needed for less formal ADR procedures.

The price of ADR services varies widely. At the American Arbitration Association, where fees are based on the stated amount of a claim, the charge can range from several hundred to many thousands of dollars. Elsewhere, neutrals' fees are based on lawyers' hourly rates, which range up to $600.

TIP: The provider should have no financial stake in the outcome, so avoid firms whose fee is linked to the size of the resulting settlement.

TIP: A neutral who's had prior (or worse yet, repeat) business from your adversary may not be impartial.

FYI: An inexpensive route to ADR is through one of the many Better Business Bureaus operated nationwide. Often disputes can be mediated free of charge and by telephone. Common claims include failure to provide the service or product promised, defective or damaged merchandise, false advertising, and breach of warranty.

As with selecting any professional, it's important to examine the credentials of an ADR provider. Here are some issues to consider before retaining a provider:

◆ How many cases has the organization handled, and what percentage of them have been resolved using ADR? You'll also want to check the track record of any neutral who might be assigned to your case. Unfortunately, you'll have no way of verifying this information. But getting the statistics and checking with a couple of former clients makes you a more informed consumer.

◆ What types of ADR techniques does the provider specialize in? The name of the organization doesn't necessarily tell you. For example, the American Arbitration Association offers a wide range of services besides arbitration.

◆ What is the background of the group's neutrals? Are they mostly retired judges? Nonlawyers?

◆ Does the business offer administered or nonadministered ADR *(see Q100)* or a combination of the two?

- Will the firm supply you with a client list and allow you to speak to other companies that have relied on the organization and the neutral who will be assigned to your case?
- Does the firm or the neutral you'd be working with have expertise in the substantive area of your dispute, whether it's franchising, patents, or construction law?
- What is the provider's fee structure?
- Does the provider guarantee that its third-party neutrals will disclose any conflicts of interest *(see Q37)* in handling your case?
- Has the neutral to be assigned to your case ever handled an ADR proceeding involving your opponent before?
- What is the complaint mechanism if you're dissatisfied with the service?

FYI: Nationwide ADR providers include the New York–based American Arbitration Association, which also offers mediation (212-484-4000), and JAMS/Endispute, based in Irvine, California. (Call 800-352-5267 to reach the office nearest you.) For independent help locating a dispute resolution service in your area or one that specializes in your industry, contact the National Institute for Dispute Resolution in Washington, D.C., at 202-466-4764.

CHAPTER 8

Record Keeping and Taxes

O MATTER HOW MUCH YOU RELY ON
your lawyer or tax adviser, no one knows your
business as well as you do. That uniquely equips
you for playing the tax game to your advantage.

On one side of the equation are the various taxes
you must pay. They depend not only on your
income but also on the kind of business you run
and who helps you do the work—employees or
independent contractors.

While the tax law takes with one hand, you
might say it gives back with the other, enabling you
to lower your bill with various deductions. The
better informed you are about what they are, the
more opportunities you can find in your own
business to trim substantial bucks off what you
owe.

Time-consuming though it seems, it also pays
to keep careful records. Should the IRS come

calling, being able to show that you stuck to the rules will be your best defense.

Write-Offs

ONE OF THE CONTINUING SURPRISES TO SOME BUSI-ness owners is just how costly running a company can be. Many of your hard-won dollars go toward paying for things that staff employees get for free, such as office space, telephone calls, and supplies. Tax deductions balance out this bleak financial picture. The more expenses you can write off, the lower your taxes, and the more money you'll take home.

WHAT ARE THE RULES ON HOME-OFFICE DEDUCTIONS?

FOR STARTERS, YOU MUST DEVOTE THE space *exclusively* to business on a regular basis. That doesn't mean you need an entire room set aside for the purpose—just that you can't use the area for other activities. For instance, if your home office doubles as a TV room, it's usually not deductible. Two exceptions: if you run a day-care facility from your home or store inventory or product samples there, you don't have to meet the "exclusive use" test.

Next, the IRS looks at the type of space and the role it plays in your business. Easiest to qualify are separate structures, such as studios, unattached garages, or barns. You can deduct the expense of these areas if you use them in your trade or business.

For other parts of your home, the rules get more stringent. The office must be either your "principal place of business" or a space where you meet clients or customers. Until recently, the law didn't define the term, "principal place of business," however. The IRS usually focused on how much time you spent in your home office and the relative importance of what you did there.

These standards proved troublesome for people who ran their businesses from home but performed most work at other locations. Doctors, professionals, computer specialists, plumbers, electricians, and other service businesses were often out of luck.

Congress substantially relaxed the rule in 1997, although the changes unfortunately weren't to take effect until two years later. Starting in 1999, your home qualifies as your principal place of business if you conduct administrative or management activities there, instead of running your company entirely from another place. The office doesn't even have to be the only one, as long as you don't conduct "substantial administrative or management activities" someplace else. Employees who want to take the home-office deduction have another hurdle. They must either use the space for the company's convenience (rather than their own) or rent to their employer the area used for work.

If you satisfy the various tests, you can write off both direct and indirect expenses of running a home office. Direct expenses, which are fully deductible, benefit only the business part of your home—painting the room that you use as an office, for example. Indirect expenses affect both the business and personal parts of the house or apartment. They include: real estate taxes, deductible mortgage interest, building depreciation, rent (if you don't own your home), utilities, insurance, repairs, and burglar alarms.

With indirect expenses, you'll need to determine how much of your home is used exclusively for business. You can make this allocation in one of two ways, says Stephen Corrick, a tax partner at Arthur Andersen in Washington, D.C. One possibility is to measure the total floor space and figure out how much of it your office occupies. Another is to add up the number of rooms and do the same type of calculation. Either way, you can deduct the portion of indirect expenses attributable to your office.

For example, let's say your house is 2,500 square feet and your office occupies 500 square feet, or 20 percent of the floor space. If your indirect expenses are $20,000 per year, you can write off $4,000 of that sum (20 percent of $20,000) for the home office.

If you own your home, there's one more bit of math to do. It involves depreciation—a gradual deduction of the value of the house (but not the land). Here, too, you'll need to know what portion of your home is used for business. Your total depreciation is that percentage times either the adjusted basis (the cost of the house plus capital improvements) when you install your home office or the fair market value at that time—whichever is less. Typically, you would spread those deductions out over 39 years.

Whether or not you actually depreciate your home, taking a home-office deduction could work against you in the event of a sale. Under the 1997 tax law, when you sell your principal residence, you pay no tax on the first $250,000 in profits ($500,000 for married couples filing jointly), provided the house was your principal residence for at least two of the five years before selling it. Although the law isn't entirely clear, many tax experts think you lose that exclusion for whatever part of the house was attributable to your office.

For example, let's say you buy a house for $200,000, use 10 percent of it as a home office, and write off those costs for

10 years. Then you sell the house for $400,000 at a profit of $200,000. Ordinarily, the entire profit would be tax free. But since you took the home office deduction, part of the house is considered business property (rather than your personal residence), and so a corresponding portion is subject to tax, says Susan Jacksack, a tax analyst with CCH, Inc., a publisher of tax and business information in Riverwoods, Illinois. And that's true whether or not you actually depreciated the office.

To figure how much tax you'd be required to pay involves a multistep calculation, Jacksack says. First, you figure your profit on the portion of the house that you used for business. In this case, the initial basis for that part of the house is $20,000 (10 percent of the $200,000 purchase price). With 39 years to fully depreciate the property, your depreciation would be roughly $513 annually ($200,000/39). In 10 years you would have taken $5,130 in depreciation, reducing the basis of the business part of the property to $14,870 ($20,000 minus $5,128). Since you used 10 percent of the house for business, $40,000 ($400,000 x 10 percent) of the sale price is attributable to business property. Your profit from selling this part of the house is therefore $25,130 ($40,000 minus your adjusted basis of $14,870).

Two different tax rates would apply to this gain. The amount of your depreciation (in this case, $5,128) is "recaptured" in the sale, and taxed at a rate of 25 percent. The other $20,000 in profit is taxed at the capital gains rate of 20 percent.

Assuming this interpretation is correct (and only time will tell whether it is), the law seems to apply to all business use of the home after May 6, 1997. So taxpayers who took home office deductions before then probably won't be taxed on depreciation claimed before May 7, 1997, says Jacksack.

Of course, the rule won't affect you if your home doesn't go up much in value or you don't expect to sell it any time soon. Otherwise, you and your tax adviser should weigh the financial pros and cons of deducting the home office. Perhaps it's worth taking the write-off to put more money in your pocket today. Another possible strategy is to stop using the home office exclusively for business three years before you plan to sell.

FYI: You can't use the home-office deduction to claim a loss: your profits from the business before figuring this expense must be more than the office costs.

WHAT TYPE OF PROPERTY CAN BE DEPRECIATED ON MY FEDERAL TAX RETURN?

Q 106 IF YOU RECENTLY MADE A CAPITAL INVESTMENT in your business, you may have a choice of taking a onetime tax deduction for the expense or depreciating it during a number of years. You'll want to pick the method most likely to reduce what you owe in taxes.

Property can be depreciated if it's used in your business or held for investment, has a determinable life that is longer than one year, and loses value by wearing out, decaying, being used up, or becoming obsolete.

Depreciable property can be *intangible* (for instance a patent, copyright, or franchise) or *tangible* (like machinery or real estate). Land is not depreciable, but structures that you own on it (such as buildings) are. You can begin depreciating in the same year you start using the property for your business. Depreciation continues until you recover your cost, dispose of the property, or stop using it for business or investment.

Under Section 179 of the tax code, all or part of the costs of some depreciable property may be *expensed*—that is, written off in a lump sum during a single tax year. Unlike the rules on depreciation, this provision covers only tangible personal property (a broad category that includes manufacturing equipment, personal computers, cellular phones, signs, and cars). Section 179 does not cover real property, so it would not include, for example, buildings or fixtures, both of which are depreciable.

In order for items to qualify for a Section 179 deduction, they must have been purchased for use in your business; or, if they were acquired for both business and personal reasons, you must use them for business more than half the time. You lose the right to a Section 179 deduction if you don't take it in the first year you use the property.

The total Section 179 deduction is limited to $18,500 for

1998 and increases gradually to $25,000 by the year 2003 ($19,000 in 1999; $20,000 in 2000; and $24,000 in 2001–2002). Additional limits apply to deductions for cars *(see Q108).*

If you're claiming the Section 179 deduction for property that costs more than $200,000, you must reduce your initial deduction by one dollar for each dollar over $200,000. Another restriction: you may not use a Section 179 deduction to create a loss; but a deduction disallowed for this reason in one year may be carried over to the next. For information about methods of depreciating or expensing different types of property, how to claim the deductions, and which forms to file, consult your tax adviser or IRS Publication 534, *Depreciation.*

TIP: Any cost not expensed may be depreciated; on your return, reduce the book value of the depreciable property to reflect the deduction you've already taken.

ARE THERE ANY TAX ADVANTAGES TO LEASING, RATHER THAN OWNING, A BUSINESS VEHICLE?

Q 107 NO, SAYS MARK GOTTLIEB, A GREAT NECK, NEW York accountant who specializes in small business. The only reason to lease is if you need (or want) to drive a new model car every two or three years.

Whether you buy or lease the vehicle, you can deduct expenses related to business use *(see Q108).* With leasing, there's a little less paperwork involved in claiming the deduction. Instead of depreciating or expensing the car *(see Q106),* as you would if you owned it, you simply multiply the yearly lease payments by the percentage of your business use. So if your payments are $6,000 per year and you use the car 60 percent for business, your deduction would be $3,600.

HOW SHOULD I DEDUCT BUSINESS USE OF MY FAMILY CAR OR TRUCK?

 PRORATE ACTUAL COSTS, COMPARE IT WITH THE standard IRS mileage allowance, and use whichever method is most favorable. But be aware that if you take the standard mileage allowance, you must do so during the first year you drive the vehicle for business. After that, you can use the standard mileage rate or deduct your actual expenses if you prefer. (If you switch to actual expenses, you'll just need to make some adjustments for depreciation, since the standard rate includes it.)

In any event, you should keep a diary of the distances you drive for business, where you go, and the purpose of each trip. Driving to your office each day is considered a commuting expense and isn't deductible. However, you can write off trips between offices (if you have more than one) and visits to clients and customers.

Record keeping is easiest with the standard mileage allowance, since you don't need to keep track of most actual expenses (business-related parking and tolls are two notable exceptions). The trouble is, the allowance at press time was a skimpy 32.5 cents per mile (rates change, so check with the IRS). Unless you drive huge distances for business, figuring your actual costs will yield a bigger write-off. One of the main attractions of deducting actual costs is being able to expense the vehicle under Section 179 *(see Q106)* during year Number One and depreciate it in subsequent years.

You can take the Section 179 write-off only in the year you buy the car and start using it for business. To be eligible for this deduction, you must use your car for business more than half the time. The IRS sets yearly limits on how much of a write-off you can take, based on what you paid for the car. To calculate the deduction, you multiply this sum by the percentage of your business use.

When claiming depreciation in subsequent years, you apply the same approach. If your business use ever drops to 50 percent or less, you'll have to pay tax on the amount you previously expensed and add that sum back into the basis of the car.

For information about methods of depreciating or expensing a car, how to claim the deductions, and which forms to file, consult your tax adviser or IRS Publication 463, *Travel, Entertainment, Gift and Car Expenses.*

Other expenses you can deduct include: garage rent, insurance, repairs, gas, oil, tolls, and tires.

If you use your car for personal as well as company purposes, you must keep track of how much you drive for business. At the end of each year, you'll add up these miles, then compare them with the total distance traveled. Your deduction will equal that percentage times all your expenses. Apply the same method to figuring depreciation.

WHAT IS THE YEARLY DEDUCTION FOR SELF-EMPLOYED HEALTH INSURANCE?

 THE TAXPAYER RELIEF ACT OF 1997 SET A schedule for gradually raising the limits. The percentage you can deduct is:

1998 through 1999	45 percent
2000 through 2001	50 percent
2002	60 percent
2003 through 2005	80 percent
2006	90 percent
2007 and later	100 percent

This deduction applies not just to business owners but also to spouses and dependents. Take the deduction on Form 1040 as an adjustment to income.

CAN EMPLOYING MY SPOUSE INCREASE MY DEDUCTION FOR HEALTH INSURANCE AND OTHER MEDICAL EXPENSES?

 YES. IF YOU CAN EMPLOY YOUR SPOUSE, YOU may be able to completely deduct health insurance costs and unreimbursed medical and dental expenses for the entire family. This approach is based on Section 105 of the Internal Revenue Code, which deals with computing taxable income. Nothing in this section says you can deduct health insurance costs by hiring your mate. But accountants, lawyers, and tax planners have figured out a way for small businesses to structure their benefits packages to do just that.

Here's how it works. You put your spouse on the payroll to perform a legitimate business function (such as bookkeeping or marketing). You pay your husband or wife wages commensurate with those services, plus fringe benefits. As part of that benefits package, you offer health insurance for the worker and family (including you), plus reimbursement for medical expenses not covered by insurance.

With this technique, you avoid the two hurdles that you must usually cross before you can write off medical and dental expenses. Typically, you must first itemize deductions on Schedule A of the tax return—which doesn't pay unless these expenses exceed the standard deduction (at press time, it was $4,150 for single people or up to $6,900 for a married couple). Assuming you meet this threshold (many people do by itemizing state, local, and real estate taxes and interest paid on a mortgage), your unreimbursed medical and dental expenses aren't deductible unless they exceed 7.5 percent of your adjusted gross income. So unless you have many doctors' bills or spend a lot of time in the dentist's chair, you probably won't qualify for the deduction.

In contrast, if you offer your spouse a benefits package, you can reimburse the first dollar of medical expenses not paid for by insurance—for your spouse and the rest of the family—subject to a reasonable cap (like $5,000 per family). This sweet deal, along with your health insurance premiums, is completely deductible to your business as an employee benefits plan. By reducing your business income, it may also shave dollars off what you owe in state and self-employment taxes *(see Q117)*.

Setting up and maintaining one of these plans requires some paperwork. Ideally, you should put in writing the spouse's responsibilities, his or her pay, and roughly how many hours a year of work you anticipate (it should average more than 10 hours per week). The U.S. Department of Labor requires that you file a summary of the plan within 90 days of setting it up and annually after that. In case of an audit, you'll want to have an adoption agreement, along with records listing medical expenses for each year and how they were handled.

FYI: AgriPlan/Bizplan, a company in Adel, Iowa, that puts together Section 105 plans for small businesses (800-626-2846), charges $175 a year to prepare these and other documents. Phil Harrington, the company president, recommends that the spouse-employee keep time sheets. Those who follow AgriPlan/Bizplan's procedures to the letter get an audit guarantee: the company says it will pay any penalty that results from a Section 105 plan it sets up.

Another piece of paperwork that you'll have to do yourself is reporting your spouse's annual wages to the IRS and paying employment taxes *(see Q116)*. To survive IRS scrutiny, Harrington recommends that the wages equal at least 20 to 30 percent of the total compensation package. So for a package worth $10,000 a year, the spouse should earn at least $2,000 to $3,000.

Of course, this approach isn't for everyone. Not only must you employ a spouse, but such a generous benefits package could get prohibitively expensive for all but the smallest Mom-and-Pops. Under the federal law known as the Employee Retirement Income Security Act (or ERISA), you can't legally discriminate in the benefits you provide to different employees. By offering a Section 105 plan to some employees, you might get stuck paying these potentially costly benefits to all.

Section 105 plans are best for business entities that employ fewer than three full-time employees, Harrington says. That includes sole proprietorships, partnerships in which the spouse isn't an owner, and limited-liability companies in which the spouse isn't also a principal.

A C-corporation owner *(see Q2)* doesn't need to employ his or her spouse to reap the benefits of Section 105; the corporation can provide the owner and family with health insurance as part of an employee benefits package that is deductible to the corporation. For a number of reasons, the savings are so minimal for S-corporations that Section 105 plans don't make sense for most of these businesses, Harrington says.

TIP: As your payroll grows, you may want to switch from a Section 105 plan, which is entirely employer funded, to a so-called Section 125 plan (also named for a section of the Internal Revenue Code). Under these "cafeteria" plans, employees select from among two or more benefits and pick up some of the costs. Choices may include health insurance, term life insurance (up to $50,000), and disability insurance. See your tax adviser for help setting up one of these packages.

WHAT IS A MEDICAL SAVINGS ACCOUNT?

Q 111 UNDER A FOUR-YEAR PILOT PROGRAM BEGUN in 1997, self-employed people and some small businesses can set up tax-exempt medical savings accounts (or MSAs) to cover costs not paid for by health insurance. Within certain limits, you can contribute to a MSA for yourself and each employee you cover. Money paid into an MSA each year is deductible from your personal income tax return, if you're self-employed, or on the "employee benefits programs" line of your business tax return.

You put the money into a special account, administered by a bank, insurance company, or other business that acts as trustee. Staff members or you (if you're self-employed) then draw upon the account to pay for medical expenses not covered by health insurance, including out-of-pocket costs before meeting the deductible and charges for eyeglasses and preventive care not covered by many insurance policies. Funds not spent at the end of a year can be carried over to the following one, tax-free, in an interest-bearing account. If an employee chooses to withdraw the money instead before age 65, the funds are usually subject to income tax plus a 15 percent penalty.

Several other restrictions apply. First, you must be self-employed or fit the definition of "small business" under the 1996 law establishing this program. For this purpose, "small business" means a company with 50 or fewer employees during either of the preceding two calendar years. New companies can qualify if they reasonably expect to employ an average of 50 workers during the current calendar year. Growing businesses can continue to qualify as long as they have 200 or fewer employees.

The second condition is that you offer an MSA in conjunction with a high-deductible health plan. Under the law, this means a plan with an annual deductible of $1,500 to $2,250 for individuals and $3,000 to $4,500 for families. This insurance must not require out-of-pocket payments of more than $3,000 for individual coverage or $5,500 for a family policy.

Provided you meet these thresholds, you can fund the MSA in any amount, up to 65 percent of the annual deductible under the policy for individuals and 75 percent of the annual deductible for families. So for an employee with family coverage and a $3,000 per year deductible, you could put $2,250 into the MSA.

When funding MSAs, you must make comparable contributions for employees in the same job category (for instance, part time or full time) or who have the same kind of coverage. That means you have to contribute the same dollar amount to each account or, under a high-deductible plan, put in the same percentage of the annual deductible.

In theory, MSAs make good business sense, particularly for people who are self-employed. You buy a high-deductible insurance plan, which costs less. Contributions to the MSA are deductible and earn interest tax-free until they're withdrawn.

But what ought to be a no-brainer for any company that qualifies has turned out to be less popular than one might expect. In fact, the 1996 law that set up this program as an experiment includes limits on how many people can participate (the cutoff is 750,000 by the year 2000). And so far the number of businesses signing up hasn't come close to the cap. The reason relates less to the law than to the practical aspects of setting up an MSA.

Unfortunately, laws in some states make it financially unattractive for insurance companies to offer these plans. Indianapolis-based Golden Rule, one of the leading companies that puts together MSAs (888-672-0829), only offers them in 27 states; California and New York are not among them. Time Insurance of Milwaukee, another big player (888-TIME-MSA), offers plans for the self-employed in 42 states (not including New York and New Jersey), and small-group plans in about 20 states. To find out who's offering these plans in your area, call the Employers Council on Flexible Compensation in Washington, D.C., at 202-842-3232.

Assuming you can find a company that offers MSAs in your area, you may be disappointed with one of the key terms it imposes: typically, these plans require that you buy your high-deductible insurance policy from the same company offering the MSA. Even if you were free to buy the underlying health insurance policy on the open market, the law sets such specific (and arbitrary) requirements for deductibles and out-of-pocket payments that you'd have a hard time finding a plan that fits within its framework.

Let's hope future changes in the law and the marketplace will correct these problems and make MSAs available to more businesses.

WHAT ARE THE MAJOR DIFFERENCES BETWEEN A SIMPLE IRA AND A SIMPLE 401(K)?

Q 112 THE SAVINGS INCENTIVE MATCH PLAN, OR SIMPLE, is a new type of retirement plan, established by the 1996 Small Business Job Protection Act and suitable for all types of business entities. Several restrictions apply: the company must have 100 or fewer employees who received at least $5,000 in compensation during the previous year; you must fund the plan each year; and if you set up a SIMPLE plan, you can't have any other kind of retirement plan.

SIMPLEs operate as salary reduction plans, meaning that employees can choose to have the company put part of their pretax earnings directly into a retirement account instead of receiving it in cash. The account can be either an IRA or a 401(k). No matter which form it takes, employees can "defer" up to $6,000 a year. The money grows tax-free until it's withdrawn.

Companies, in turn, must make a contribution, which is deductible to the business and not taxable to the employee. This may be either a dollar-for-dollar match, limited to 3 percent of each worker's compensation or a flat, 2 percent of compensation for all "eligible" employees (those who earn at least $5,000 a year).

Only $160,000 of a worker's pay (indexed for inflation) is taken into account in figuring the company's mandatory contribution and maximum annual additions for a SIMPLE 401(k). The SIMPLE IRA rules don't have that limit. Therefore, a highly paid executive can get a higher match from the company using a SIMPLE IRA, says Joan Vines, national director of employee benefits tax services at Grant Thornton in Washington, D.C. This is a key difference between a SIMPLE plan that operates as an IRA and one that's a 401(k).

Take the case of an employee earning $200,000 a year. If that person funded a SIMPLE IRA to the maximum level, he or she could contribute $6,000, Vines says, with the company matching 3 percent, or another $6,000, to bring the total yearly contribution to $12,000.

In contrast, the same person funding a SIMPLE 401(k) could only work from a base of $160,000 in calculating the company's maximum contribution. The most that person could contribute would be $6,000, plus a company match of an additional $4,800 (3 percent of $160,000), for a total of $10,800, Vines says.

The SIMPLE IRA also works out better for lower-level employees, Vines says. With a SIMPLE 401(k), the total annual additions (through salary reductions and the company match) can't exceed 25 percent of the worker's compensation. So an employee must be earning at least $27,275 to take advantage of the full $6,000 elective deferral and still get a company match. In this case, the match would only be $818 though ($27,275 x 3 percent), since the total annual additions can't be more than $6,819 (25 percent of $27,275).

In contrast, with a SIMPLE IRA, any employee earning at least $6,000 can choose to defer the maximum of $6,000 and still get a 3 percent company match. So a worker who earns just $6,000 can defer that entire amount and get a company match of $180 (3 percent of $6,000), for a total of $6,180.

Businesses that adopt SIMPLE IRAs also get a break for their required contributions. The company can decrease its matching contribution to as little as 1 percent during two out of five years.

Plus, there's far less yearly paperwork involved than there is with a SIMPLE 401(k). For a SIMPLE 401(k), the company must maintain a written plan document and is generally required to file an annual report (Form 5500) with the IRS. This form isn't required for the SIMPLE IRA, though the company or IRA trustee must fulfill certain employee notification requirements.

A SIMPLE 401(k) would be attractive to a company that wants to limit its match for highly compensated employees to $4,800 while offering staff the option of making the maximum contribution allowed. Otherwise, the ease of administration and flexibility about funding make the SIMPLE IRA a much better choice.

WHAT ARE THE MAJOR DIFFERENCES BETWEEN A KEOGH AND A SEP-IRA?

 BOTH TYPES OF RETIREMENT PLANS CAN WORK well for people who are self-employed, partners, or members of limited-liability companies. The accounts are funded by the company, which can deduct the contribution. Earnings are tax-free to the employee until the money is withdrawn.

How should you decide which plan is better for you? Generally speaking, the SEP-IRA (Simplified Employee Pension) is easier to adopt and administer, but you can't sock away as much money tax-free. The maximum yearly contribution to a SEP-IRA is 15 percent of compensation or $24,000 (indexed for inflation), whichever is less.

In contrast, if you play your cards right, you can put up to 25 percent of compensation into a Keogh. You have the choice of a *profit-sharing plan,* a *money-purchase pension,* or a combination of the two. In calculating how much you can contribute to your own account, you must figure your compensation before the deduction for self-employment tax *(see Q117)* and your own contributions to the plan.

With a *profit-sharing plan,* contributions can vary from one year to the next, depending on how well your company does. The maximum contribution is the smaller of $30,000 or 15 percent of taxable compensation for employees and the smaller of $30,000 or 13.0435 percent of taxable compensation for self-employed people. Only $160,000 of compensation (indexed for inflation) is taken into account in figuring the contribution.

In a *money-purchase pension,* you must contribute a fixed percentage of participants' compensation each year (determined when you set up the plan), whether or not the company is prospering; you can't fund your own account, though, unless you show a profit. Here the maximum contribution is the smaller of $30,000 or 25 percent of taxable compensation for employees and the smaller of $30,000 or 20 percent of taxable compensation for people who are self-employed. Again, only $160,000 of compensation (indexed for inflation) is taken into account in figuring the contribution.

By maintaining a profit-sharing plan and a money-purchase pension, you can fund your Keogh in the maximum amount while leaving yourself free to vary at least part of your contribution—depending on profits. You would do that by putting a fixed percentage each year into the money-purchase pension. The rest of your contribution, to bring the total to 25 percent, would go into the profit-sharing plan and could vary from year to year.

Though attractive for single-owner businesses, both SEP-IRAs and Keoghs get expensive once your staff starts to grow, Joan Vines notes. That's because federal rules generally require that if you fund these plans for one person, you must fund them at the same level (for instance, the same percentage in a money-purchase pension) for everyone. As your staff expands, you might want to switch to another, less costly type of retirement plan. This might be a SIMPLE IRA or a SIMPLE 401(k) *(see Q112).*

TIP: Some Keoghs lock you into funding the plan each year. With a SEP-IRA, you can wait to see how well your business goes. This feature makes the SEP-IRA more attractive than certain Keoghs.

FYI: Under recent changes in the law, new SEP-IRAs can no longer operate as so-called "elective deferral" or salary reduction plans, in which workers ask that a portion of their pretax pay be put directly into the retirement account. The new rules only permit employer funding of the account (SEP-IRAs set up before December 31, 1996, can continue to operate as salary reduction plans.)

WHEN CAN I CLAIM A BAD DEBT DEDUCTION?

 YOU CAN'T TAKE THIS DEDUCTION UNLESS you've already reported the money due as income. The next question is whether the debt is really "bad." The answer depends not on how long the money is overdue but on whether you'll ever get paid. In general, you must have tried all the usual collection methods first *(see Q88–89)*. Proof that a company has filed for bankruptcy and that you're not a secured or preferred creditor *(see Q93)* usually shows that a debt is worthless.

WHAT OTHER BUSINESS EXPENSES CAN I DEDUCT ON MY FEDERAL TAX RETURN?

TO SOME EXTENT, THE ANSWER DEPENDS ON your business. You're allowed to deduct "ordinary and necessary" expenses. "Ordinary" means common and accepted in your business, trade, or profession. "Necessary" means helpful and appropriate for your business, trade, or profession—it doesn't have to be indispensable. Here are some potential deductions:

◆ **Advertising.** This includes the cost of public service advertising if you reasonably expect it will bring you business.

◆ **Dues for membership in trade and professional associations, including chambers of commerce.**

◆ **Education expenses.** Two types of education expenses may be deductible. One category involves training your employees.

The other includes classes you take yourself. These may be required by law or necessary to maintain or improve skills in your current work. What you can't deduct is education to meet the minimum requirements of your present trade, business, or profession or to qualify you for a new one. When the write-off is permitted, it covers not just tuition but also books, supplies, and transportation.

◆ **Gifts of up to $25 per person during a single tax year.**

◆ **Insurance premiums.** This includes premiums for property and liability insurance; workers' comp; life insurance for your employees, provided you're not the beneficiary; and health insurance for your staff. Depending on your company structure and benefits plan, you may be able to deduct the premiums for self-employed health insurance *(see Q109)* or write off the cost of health insurance available under an employee benefits plan *(see Q110)*.

◆ **Legal and professional fees.** This usually includes book-keeping expenses, lawyers' bills, and fees to prepare the business part of your tax return.

◆ **Office rent, repairs, and cleaning.**

◆ **Postage and shipping charges.**

◆ **Repairs and maintenance of business equipment.** You can deduct expenses to keep your property operating normally and efficiently (including labor and parts). The cost of improving business equipment must be capitalized *(see Q106)*.

◆ **Subscriptions to trade or professional journals in your field.**

◆ **Supplies and materials.** Those used in manufacturing are charged to the cost of goods sold. Otherwise you can deduct supplies as a business expense.

◆ **Taxes and licenses.** These include state and local licenses and regulatory fees for your trade or business, as well as the following taxes: real estate taxes on business property, state and local income taxes on the business entity (such as those sometimes imposed on corporations, partnerships, or unincorporated businesses), employment taxes *(see Q116)*, and excise taxes *(see Q119)*.

◆ **Travel, meals, and entertainment.** You can generally deduct expenses for yourself and your employees when business travel takes you away from home. Deductible expenses include transportation, lodging, meals, cleaning, tips, and business telephone calls. The cost of entertaining clients, customers, and employees is usually only 50 percent deductible.

♦ **Utilities and telephone.** Bills for heat, power, and light are all deductible. So is your business use of the telephone *(see Q123).*

♦ **Wages paid to employees.** Salaries are deductible if you can show they were "ordinary and necessary," reasonable, and paid for services actually performed.

Taxes

WHAT TAX OBLIGATIONS DOES MY COMPANY HAVE IF I EMPLOY OTHER PEOPLE?

 FOR PEOPLE WHO ARE YOUR EMPLOYEES, rather than independent contractors *(see Q54),* you're required to withhold or pay certain taxes, sometimes called collectively "payroll taxes." Penalties may apply if you don't withhold the taxes, if you withhold them but don't turn them over to the government, or if you pay the Feds late. So even if you're short of cash, resist the temptation to "borrow" from withheld taxes rather than paying the money on time to the government.

These are the tax rules you need to be aware of:

♦ **Federal income tax withholding.** You must withhold tax from employees' paychecks and deposit it with an authorized financial institution or a Federal Reserve Bank for your area. When you hire employees, have them fill out Form W-4, indicating their filing status and number of withholding allowances. You can use that information to calculate how much income tax to withhold. In addition, both you and your workers need to complete Form I-9, "Employment Eligibility Verification." This form, which you can get from the Immigration and Naturalization Service (800-755-0777), verifies that an employee is legally eligible to work in the United States.

At the end of each year, you must give every employee a

Form W-2, indicating total wages, tips, and other compensation, along with the Social Security and Medicare taxes you've withheld. You also need to send a copy of this form to the Social Security Administration.

◆ **Social Security and Medicare taxes.** These taxes pay for benefits under the Federal Insurance Contributions Act (or FICA). You withhold the worker's portion of these taxes and pay a matching amount, which is deductible as a business expense. To find out how much, refer to IRS Publication 15, Circular E, *Employer's Tax Guide.* Report these taxes quarterly, along with income tax withheld, on Form 941, "Employer's Quarterly Federal Tax Return." Unless you deposit taxes electronically, use Form 8109 to send them in before you file Form 941. You must deposit both your part and the employee's part of Social Security and Medicare taxes.

◆ **Federal Unemployment Tax (FUTA).** This is part of the federal and state program that pays unemployment compensation to people who lose their jobs. If you're also required to pay state unemployment tax, you get a credit for it against what you owe the Feds. If you employ your spouse in your business *(see Q110),* you must withhold income tax on his or her wages and pay Social Security and Medicare, but you're not required to pay unemployment tax.

Report federal unemployment tax using Form 940, "Employer's Annual Federal Unemployment (FUTA) Tax Return," or the shortened version, 940-EZ, due January 31. (Refer to Publication 15 to see if you can use this simplified version.) Unless you pay taxes electronically, use Form 8109 to make deposits, which are usually due on April 30, July 31, October 31, and January 31. If you owe $100 or less, you can wait until the next quarter to deposit these taxes.

WHO HAS TO PAY SELF-EMPLOYMENT TAX?

Q 117 THIS IS A TAX THAT SELF-EMPLOYED PEOPLE must pay to cover Social Security and Medicare. While staff employees also contribute to the system, the company they work for picks up half. Self-employed people must pay the whole thing themselves. At press time, the rate was 15.3 percent (12.4 percent for Social Security and

2.9 percent for Medicare). The cap on earnings for 1998 subject to Social Security is $68,400.

Those businesses required to pay self-employment tax have profits of at least $400. Among them are: sole proprietors, partners, independent contractors *(see Q54)*, and some members of limited-liability companies who are active in the company's operations. In figuring self-employment income, people with more than one company would combine the net income from the two businesses.

If you operate as a C-corporation *(see Q2)* and are technically an employee, you don't need to pay the tax, but if you're a corporate director and receive fees for that service, it counts as self-employment income. Shareholders in an S-corporation don't pay self-employment tax on their share of the corporation's taxable income. Nor do those who are also officers of the corporation and perform services for the company; they're treated as employees, subject to withholding for Social Security and Medicare.

Compute your self-employment tax on Form SE and attach it to your federal tax return, Form 1040. If you're discouraged about what it adds up to, take heart: one-half the self-employment tax is deductible on Form 1040 as an adjustment to income.

FYI: You're required to pay self-employment tax even if you have a "day job" and operate your business on the side. In that case, your employer would withhold Social Security and Medicare from your paycheck and you would pay self-employment tax on any outside earnings.

WHEN DO I HAVE TO PAY ESTIMATED TAXES?

IF YOUR BUSINESS HAS PROFITS OF AT LEAST $1,000 a year, you must make estimated payments every quarter. Small businesses operating as C-corporations *(see Q2)* calculate this tax on Form 1120-W (worksheet) and use Form 8109 *(see Q12)* to deposit it with the Feds.

Sole proprietors, partners, S-corporation shareholders, and limited-liability company members who pay tax at individual rates *(see Q1)* need to file Form 1040-ES. You must generally pay at least 90 percent of what you owe during the year or 100 percent of what you owed for all 12 months of the previous year, whichever is smaller.

To figure your tax, estimate net earnings as well as you can. Then subtract credits, exemptions, and anticipated deductions. Adjustments to income, like contributions to retirement plans *(see Q113)* and the self-employed health insurance deduction *(see Q109)*, can help reduce your bill. But don't forget to add in self-employment tax *(see Q117)* if you have to pay it. IRS Form 1040-ES, which includes vouchers to file with your payment, has a worksheet to guide you through the math. For help completing the form, you can also refer to IRS Publication 505, *Tax Withholding and Estimated Tax.*

To avoid a penalty, make payments on the 15th day of the fourth, sixth, and ninth months of your fiscal year, and on the 15th day of the first month of the following fiscal year. If your tax year coincides with the calendar year, that means:

FOR MONEY RECEIVED	ESTIMATED TAX DUE
January 1 through March 31	April 15
April 1 through May 31	June 15
June 1 through August 31	September 15
September 1 through December 31	January 15 of the following year

FYI: As a rule, you're required to pay what you owe in four equal installments, but you get a break if your income isn't spread evenly throughout the year. Assuming you have no profits during the first quarter, for instance, you won't owe any tax for that installment. By the same token, if earnings for the first quarter are higher than for any other, your initial payment must reflect it.

WHAT ARE EXCISE TAXES AND WHO HAS TO PAY THEM?

 THESE TAXES APPLY TO COMPANIES THAT MANU-
facture or sell certain products (like guns, tobacco,
or alcohol), operate some kinds of businesses
(such as betting pools or lotteries), or use particular equipment or products (for example, ozone-depleting chemicals).
Most small businesses don't have to worry about excise taxes.
But to be on the safe side, check with your lawyer or tax
adviser or refer to IRS Publication 510, *Excise Taxes.*

Records

IF THE THOUGHT OF A NOTICE FROM THE IRS MAKES YOU
break out in a cold sweat, you're not alone. But if you play by
the rules and keep ample records, you have nothing to fear
except inconvenience.

WHO NEEDS AN "EMPLOYER IDENTIFICATION NUMBER"?

THIS IS A NINE-DIGIT NUMBER THAT THE IRS
uses to process information it receives from you
and others, including businesses that pay you
$600 or more a year *(see Q121).* Don't let the name mislead
you: an employer identification number (or EIN) is a requirement not only if you if you have employees but also if you set
up a Keogh plan *(see Q113)* or operate as a corporation, partnership, or limited-liability company.

It takes about a month to get an EIN by filing IRS Form
SS-4 (for a copy of the form, call 800-TAX-FORM). You can
get an EIN assigned to you immediately by calling one of the
numbers listed on SS-4, but you'll still need to mail (or fax)
the form to the IRS. Otherwise, if you need to give an EIN
for some purpose (such as filing your taxes) before yours
comes through, you can usually just write "applied for" on
whatever paperwork calls for an EIN.

You must get a new EIN if you switch your company format (for instance, by converting from a sole proprietorship
to a limited-liability company) or buy an existing business

Key Tax Dates and the Forms to File

SOME OF THE TAXES you may have to pay when operating as a sole proprietor, corporation, or partnership

TAX	ENTITY
Income Tax	Sole Proprietor
Income Tax	Individual who is a partner or a S-corporation shareholder
Income Tax	C-corporation
Income Tax	S-corporation
Self-employment tax	Sole proprietor or individual who is a partner
Estimated tax	Sole proprietor or individual who is a partner or S-corporation shareholder
Estimated tax	C-corporation
Paying Social Security and Medicare taxes (FICA) and withholding income tax	Sole proprietor, C-corporation, S-corporation, or partnership
Providing information about Social Security and Medicare taxes (FICA) and withholding of income tax	Sole proprietor, C-corporation, S-corporation, or partnership
Federal Unemployment Tax	Sole proprietor, C-corporation, S-corporation, or partnership
Information about payments to nonemployees	Sole proprietor, C-corporation, S-corporation, or partnership

FORM	DUE DATE
Schedule C or C-EZ	File with Form 1040
1040	15th day of 4th month after end of entity's tax year
1120 or 1120-A	15th day of 3rd month after end of entity's tax year
1120S	15th day of 3rd month after end of entity's tax year
Schedule SE	File with Form 1040
1040ES	15th day of 4th, 6th, and 9th months of entity's tax year, and 15th day of 1st month after end of entity's tax year
1120-W (worksheet)	15th day of 4th, 6th, 9th, and 12th months of entity's tax year
941	April 30, July 31, October 31, and January 31
W-2 to employee	January 31
W-2 and W-3 to Social Security Administration	Last day of February
940 or 940-EZ	January 31
Form 8109 to make deposits	April 30, July 31, October 31, and January 31, but only if liability for unpaid tax Is more than $100
1099-MISC	January 31 to the recipient February 28 to the IRS

that you operate as a sole proprietorship. (With corporations, the EIN stays with the company if it's sold.) You'll also need a separate EIN for each Keogh plan that you start, for instance if you have both a profit-sharing plan and a money-purchase pension *(see Q113)*. It's not necessary to get a different EIN if you just change your company name.

Five or six weeks after you receive your EIN, the IRS should send you a book of Form 8109 coupons. If you're required to pay employment tax *(see Q116)* or to withhold federal income tax from workers' paychecks *(see Q116)*, you will use these coupons to deposit the payments with an authorized financial institution or a Federal Reserve Bank in your area.

FYI: *Understanding Your EIN,* a free pamphlet available from the IRS, includes step-by-step instructions for various business entities about how to complete the EIN application form.

WHAT ARE THE REQUIREMENTS FOR REPORTING PAYMENTS TO CONSULTANTS?

Q 121 IF YOU PAID A CONSULTANT, FREELANCER, lawyer, or independent contractor *(see Q54)* $600 or more during the year, you must report this information to the IRS. The form to use is 1099-MISC, "Miscellaneous Income," which is due to the individual by January 31 of the year after you pay the money and must be filed with the IRS by February 28. The form calls for the recipient's Social Security or employer identification number *(see Q120)*, so it's best to have the number on file before making any payments. You can get this information by asking freelancers to fill out Form W-9, "Request for Taxpayer Identification Number and Certification," available from the IRS.

TIP: If you're a consultant yourself, check all 1099-MISC forms that clients send you. The IRS compares the forms it receives with what you report on your tax return, so you'll want to clear up any discrepancies. (Both you and the IRS should receive any corrections.)

WHAT KINDS OF DOCUMENTATION OF BUSINESS EXPENSES DO I NEED?

Q 122 IN MOST CASES, THE IRS SIMPLY REQUIRES THAT you maintain good enough records for preparing your tax return. A useful starting point is an account book or diary showing income and expenses for the year. If you keep your books by hand, *Small Time Operator*, by Bernard Kamoroff, an accountant and small-business owner (Bell Springs Publishing, $16.95), can guide you through the process. Accounting software, like *QuickBooks Pro*, by Intuit, is a more high-tech option. It's available in both Windows and Mac versions at a "street price" of about $170.

Also, save supporting documents, such as 1099-MISC forms *(see Q121)* for money you received and receipts for expenses of more than $75. Your records may include sales slips, paid bills, credit card receipts, and cancelled checks. You should file these materials by year and type of income or expense.

You'll want to keep all records for as long as the IRS can dispute your tax return. This statute of limitations is usually three years after you file your return, though there are exceptions. For example, if the IRS claims that you underreported your gross income by more than 25 percent, the period of limitations is six years. For claims due to bad debt deductions *(see Q114)*, it's seven years. And if the IRS makes the case that your return was fraudulent, there's no limit on how long they can go after you.

Sometimes the law, or just good judgment, require you to save other documents for longer than the three-year minimum. For instance, you must keep employment tax records for at least four years after the date the tax becomes due or is paid—whichever is later.

While you're depreciating assets *(see Q106)*, you'll want to save records from prior years to help you figure the latest deduction. Even once you've finished writing off the asset, hang onto records until the period of limitations has expired for the last year of depreciation. Before you finally toss those documents, consider whether you might ever need them for insurance purposes.

FYI: If you're under audit *(see Q125)*, keep all records relevant to that audit and for all subsequent years until the audit's concluded, advises Donald Alexander, a former IRS commissioner who's now a lawyer with Akin, Gump, Strauss, Hauer & Feld in Washington, D.C.

DOES THE IRS REQUIRE ME TO HAVE SEPARATE RECORDS OF MY BUSINESS AND PERSONAL EXPENSES?

SINCE ONLY BUSINESS EXPENSES ARE DEDUCTible on your tax return, it's important to separate them from personal ones.

For most business owners, the easiest way to do this is with separate checking accounts (which the IRS requires for corporations and partnerships). Sole proprietors generally have the option of maintaining just a personal account—and often do so to avoid higher minimum balances and service charges that some banks apply for business accounts. If you maintain just one account, it's usually best to keep separate records of nonbusiness expenses. And if you use just one charge or credit card for all purchases, keep separate records of the personal expenditures.

When paying expenses that are partly personal and partly business, indicate in your records how they're divided. Special restrictions may apply. In the case of cars and trucks, for example, there are generally two choices: prorating all your vehicle costs (including gas, registration fees, and parking) or taking the IRS's standard allowance *(see Q108)*. If you work at home, typically the basic charges for the first telephone line are not deductible, but you can deduct the expense of a second line used exclusively for business. Some home-office owners find that using one long-distance carrier for business calls and another for personal ones makes it easier to separate them.

WHAT BUSINESS PRACTICES PUT ME AT RISK OF AN AUDIT?

Q 124 PROVIDED YOU KEEP THOROUGH BUSINESS records *(see Q122)* to back up your return, you have very little to fear from an audit, says Donald Alexander, the former IRS commissioner. So worrying about an audit shouldn't stop you from taking deductions you're really entitled to. These are some red flags to auditors, according to Alexander and other tax pros:

◆ Omitted income.

◆ Disproportionately large deductions (for instance, for travel, meals, and entertainment).

◆ Business losses that aren't adequately explained.

◆ Bad debt deductions *(see Q114)*.

◆ Deduction of a home office *(see Q105)*.

◆ Write-offs of personal living expenses as business expenses.

◆ Your occupation. Periodically the IRS targets certain types of businesses for audits. Farmers and gambling businesses have been two of their favorite subjects.

◆ A past audit of your own return that showed you cheated or didn't keep adequate records.

◆ The audit of customers or clients who do a lot of business in cash. If they're deducting expenses paid for in cash and you're receiving some of that dough, the IRS may check to see that you're declaring everything.

◆ An audit of another company's return prepared by your accountant that suggests the tax preparer tends to pad expenses.

TIP: Keep tax matters to yourself, Alexander advises. Each year a certain number of audits stem from disgruntled former employees, neighbors, and others who squeal. "It's dumb to cheat," he says. But it's even dumber to confide in others or even brag about your cheating. "It's amazing how many people do."

WHAT SHOULD I EXPECT IF I'M AUDITED AND HOW CAN I MINIMIZE THE PAIN?

Q 125 IF YOU'RE LUCKY, THE IRS WILL HAVE A SMALL handful of questions (for instance, about the business expenses you've deducted) and you'll be able to respond by mail or by meeting with an agent at one of the agency's offices. Far more extensive—and intrusive—is what's known as a field audit. This may be done in your accountant's office (if a tax preparer did the return for you) or at your own. Either way, you'll want to prepare by gathering all records to back up your return *(see Q122)*.

When an accountant has prepared the return, have him or her represent you. Otherwise, you might choose to handle the audit yourself. If you go that route, keep your cool and be cooperative. Answer the auditor's questions, but don't volunteer any information or rattle on, Alexander advises. Should an agent make demands that are impossible to meet, it's okay to point that out, he says.

Even if the audit's done at your company, there are some steps you can take to help prevent the agent from going overboard. In their book, *How to Defend Yourself Against the IRS* (Simon & Schuster, $16.95), Robert S. Fink and Sandor Frankel recommend you set the agent up in a separate room away from the center of activity and where you keep your books. Without looking as if you have something to hide, designate one person—your accountant or a trusted employee—to field questions and requests for records, advise the authors, who are both tax trial lawyers. Have that person bring records to the agent, retrieve them when the agent is done, and handle requests for photocopying (don't give the agent access to the copy machine).

FYI: *Tax Savvy for Small Business,* by Frederick W. Daily (Nolo Press, $26.95), is a thorough guide to the subject authored by a clever tax lawyer, who also happens to write in plain English. Part 6 includes extensive advice about dealing with the IRS, including ideas about how to handle an audit, negotiate payments, and reduce interest and penalties.

Resources

Legal Aids

American Bar Association

312-988-5000

Too bad this massive, national lawyers' trade association isn't more helpful, but sheer size seems to get in the way. Unfortunately they don't run a referral service but will direct callers to the nearest local bar association that does. If you're trying to locate a specialist in a particular area of the law and don't mind making a few phone calls, you can ask if the ABA has a committee devoted to the subject (most likely it does). Then find out who on that panel practices in your area.

HALT: An Organization of Americans for Legal Reform

202-887-8255

This consumer-oriented group with a funny name is one of the few organizations that looks out for clients, rather than lawyers. Though more oriented toward individual (rather than business) needs, the organization distributes several of its own books that small-business owners may find helpful: *Using a Lawyer . . . And What To Do If Things Go Wrong*, by Kay Ostberg ($8.95); *If You Want to Sue a Lawyer*, by Kay Ostberg ($10) (including a directory of lawyers specializing in such cases); and *Small Claims Court—Making Your Way Through the System: A Step-By-Step Guide*, by Theresa Meehan Rudy ($8.95).

Martindale-Hubbell Law Directory

This is the most complete source of lawyers' names, listing attorneys by state and by area of practice. The multivolume reference book is available in many public libraries, but Internet users will find it much more convenient to use Martindale-Hubbell on-line (http://www.martindale.com).

Periodicals

NEW LAWS AND COURT CASES CREATE AN EVER-CHANGING
landscape for small-business owners. You'll find articles
about them in the mainstream press, in careers publications,
and in magazines devoted exclusively to a small-business
audience.

In the first category, watch for occasional coverage in
Forbes, Fortune, and *Business Week* of legal issues that concern large and small companies. *The Wall Street Journal's*
"Enterprise" column, devoted exclusively to small business,
sometimes covers legal topics as well.

Workplace-oriented publications, which address self-
employment as an alternative to corporate life, also occasionally run stories with legal angles for small business owners.
You can find such coverage in *National Business Employment
Weekly* and *Fast Company,* for example.

Magazines targeted to small business include *Home
Office Computing,* which chiefly addresses the concerns of
sole proprietors, and *Entrepreneur Magazine* and *Inc.,*
which speak to slightly larger companies. All periodically
run articles on legal issues. An electronic version of *Home
Office Computing* is available to America Online users (Keyword: "soho" or "hoc") or on the Internet at http://www.
curtco.com. *Entrepreneur* and *Inc.* can also be accessed on
the World Wide Web at http://www.entrepreneurmag.com
and http://www.inc.com, respectively.

Several membership organizations with small business
constituents also have their own publications which run articles on legal matters. These include *IB,* the bimonthly magazine of the National Federation of Independent Business
(202-554-9000); *Nation's Business,* published by the U.S.
Chamber of Commerce; *Your Company,* which goes to
American Express Card holders who are small business
owners; and *Self-Employed America,* a quarterly newsletter of
the National Association for the self-employed (800-232-
NASE).

Books and Software

HERE'S WHERE TO FIND THE PUBLISHERS MENTIONED IN
this book.

Acrobat Books
P.O. Box 870
Venice, CA 90294
310-578-1055

Bell Springs Publishing
P.O. Box 1240
Willits, CA 95490
800-515-8050

Bloomberg Press
100 Business Park Drive
P.O. Box 888
Princeton, NJ 08542-0888
609-279-4670

HALT
1612 K Street, NW, Suite 510
Washington, DC 20006
202-887-8255

Harvard University Press
79 Garden Street
Cambridge, MA 02138
800-448-2242

Intuit
P.O. Box 7850
Mountain View, CA 94039
800-446-8848

Jian
1975 West El Camino Real
Suite 301
Mountain View, CA 94040
800-346-5426

Martindale-Hubbell
P.O. Box 1001
Summit, NJ 07902
800-526-4902

Merritt Publishing
1661 Ninth Street
Santa Monica, CA 90404
800-638-7597

Nolo Press
950 Parker Street
Berkeley, CA 94710
800-992-6656

Penguin
375 Hudson Street
New York, NY 10014
800-526-0275

Simon & Schuster
1230 Avenue of the Americas
New York, NY 10020
800-223-2336

IRS Forms and Publications

MOST OF THE TAX FORMS REFERRED TO IN THIS BOOK, AS WELL
as helpful IRS publications, can be downloaded from the
agency's user-friendly Web site (http://www.irs.ustreas.gov).
They are also available free by calling 800-TAX-FORM. IRS
publications are a lot simpler to read than the tax code, but
they, too, vary in clarity and complexity. Here are some you
may find useful:

15 Circular E, *Employer's Tax Guide*
334 *Tax Guide for Small Business*
463 *Travel, Entertainment, Gift and Car Expenses*
505 *Tax Withholding and Estimated Tax*
510 *Excise Taxes*
533 *Self-Employment Tax*
534 *Depreciation*
535 *Business Expenses*
560 *Retirement Plans for the Self-Employed*
583 *Starting a Business and Keeping Records*
590 *Individual Retirement Arrangements (IRAs)*

Intellectual Property

IF YOU'RE REGISTERING A COPYRIGHT, PATENT, OR TRADE-
mark, you'll want to have these phone numbers and Internet
addresses handy:

Copyrights. For a live person to answer questions, call the
Copyrights Office 202-707-0600. To order forms, call 202-
707-3000 or download them from the agency's Web site at
http://lcweb.loc.gov/copyright.

Patents and Trademarks. Live help is available from the
Patent and Trademark Office by dialing 703-308-9000. The
agency also has an extensive Web site at (http://www.uspto.
gov), including forms and publications.

Permissions and Credits

THE AUTHOR GRATEFULLY ACKNOWLEDGES THE FOLLOWING
publishers, organizations, and individuals for permission to
reproduce copyrighted material. This page constitutes a continuation of the copyright page.

Index

241

versus alternative dispute resolution, 180–81
reducing expenses, 88–89
versus settlement, 181–83
LLC. *See* limited-liability company
location, company, 2–3, 21–27
losses, deducting from taxable gains, 12

M

mail-order sales, 150–51
marketing, 141–48
Martin, Dennis, 47, 48
mediation, 117, 185–86
    business agreement clauses, 192–93
medical savings accounts (MSAs), 211–13
Medicare taxes, 220, 224–25
Menendez, Kenneth, 78
minitrial, 187–89
    business agreement clauses, 192–93
monitoring, workplace, 124–26
Mooney, Sean, 35, 37, 38–39
moonlighting, 121–22
MSAs. *See* medical savings accounts

N

Naeve, Robert, 105, 106
names
    company, changing, 17
    Internet domain, trademark for, 56–57
**National Resource Center for Consumers of Legal
    Services,** 84
negotiation, 183–85
    business agreement clauses, 192–93
    step, 191
nepotism. *See* antinepotism
noncompete agreement, 58–59
nonsolicitation agreement, 58

O

on-line legal advice, 78, 80–82, 186
overtime pay, 120–21

S

T

...nberg

Abfg L.P., founded in 1981, is a global information services, news,
...nd media company. Headquartered in New York, the company has nine
sales offices, two data centers, and 80 news bureaus worldwide.

Bloomberg Financial Markets, serving customers in 100 countries around
the world, holds a unique position within the financial services industry by providing an unparalleled combination of news, information, and analytic tools in
a single package known as the BLOOMBERG® service. Corporations, banks,
money management firms, financial exchanges, insurance companies, and
many other entities and organizations rely on Bloomberg as their primary source
of information.

BLOOMBERG NEWS℠, founded in 1990, offers worldwide coverage of
economies, companies, industries, governments, financial markets, politics,
and sports. The news service is the main content provider for Bloomberg's
broadcast media, which include BLOOMBERG TELEVISION®—the 24-hour
cable television network available in ten languages worldwide—and
BLOOMBERG NEWS RADIO™—an international radio network anchored
by flagship station BLOOMBERG NEWS RADIO AM 1130℠ in New York.

In addition to the BLOOMBERG PRESS® line of books, Bloomberg pub-
lishes *BLOOMBERG®* Magazine and *BLOOMBERG PERSONAL
FINANCE™*.

To learn more about Bloomberg, call a sales representative at:

Frankfurt:	49-69-920-410
Hong Kong:	852-2521-3000
London:	44-171-330-7500
New York:	1-212-318-2000
Princeton:	1-609-279-3000
San Francisco:	1-415-912-2960
São Paulo:	5511-3048-4500
Singapore:	65-226-3000
Sydney:	61-29-777-8686
Tokyo:	81-3-3201-8900

About the Author

Deborah L. Jacobs is a lawyer who made the switch journalism a dozen years ago and has run her own small business almost ever since. As a business writer specializing in legal topics, she covers law as it affects small business, personal finance, and workplace issues. Ms. Jacobs has been a frequent contributor to *The New York Times* and has written for many other national publications. She was the legal columnist for *Your Company* and for *Dun & Bradstreet's D & B Reports*, both magazines targeted to small businesses. She is the former editor of *Alternatives to the High Cost of Litigation*, a monthly newsletter about how companies can keep legal disputes out of court. For several years, she also wrote a nationally syndicated weekly newspaper column called "Working Life," advising workers on how to survive in today's volatile business climate. A native of New York and a graduate of Barnard College, Ms. Jacobs received her J.D. degree from Columbia Law School and M.S. from the Columbia Graduate School of Journalism. She lives in New York City with her husband and son.